I AM

David

JIMMY EVANS

— I AM —

David

10 LESSONS IN

GREATNESS FROM ISRAEL'S

MOST FAMOUS KING

GATEWAY® PRESS

ISBN: 978-1-951227-22-7
eBook ISBN: 978-1-951227-23-4

We hope you hear from the Holy Spirit and receive God's richest blessings from this Bible by Gateway Press. We want to provide the highest quality resources that take the messages, music, and media of Gateway Church to the world. For more information on other resources from Gateway Publishing®, go to gatewaypublishing.com.

Gateway Press, an imprint of Gateway Publishing
700 Blessed Way
Southlake, TX 76092
gatewaypublishing.com

Printed in the United States of America

20 21 22 23 — 5 4 3 2 1

DEDICATION

I DEDICATE THIS book to all the mighty men and women God has put in my life. I simply could not have made the journey or fought my life's battles without these wise and brave people around me. They have held up my arms, encouraged me, counseled me, and given immeasurable support and blessings in both good times and bad.

The list would be too long to include everyone—but these are those fellow warriors closest to me whom the Lord has used to strengthen and bless me:

My precious wife, Karen, and our children and their spouses: Julie and Cory Albracht and Brenton and Stephanie Evans.

I am forever grateful for Robert Morris and the elders of Gateway Church; John Andersen, Jenny Morgan, and Craig Dunnagan and the rest of the Gateway Publishing team. You guys do such excellent work!

CONTENTS

INTRODUCTION

Do you want to be great? Most of us would answer *Yes, yes, of course, I do.* I also want you to be great, so I wrote this book. I believe a great God formed you in your mother's womb, and He never creates anyone to live in mediocrity or failure. Despite any problems in your past or obstacles in your present, I believe you can achieve God's plan for greatness.

In these pages, I have laid down some stepping stones or lessons on the pathway to greatness. They aren't my stones; I simply found them and want to show them to you. In this book, you are going to be reading about a truly great man—King David of Israel. As you will soon discover, his life was far from perfect, but that didn't keep him from greatness. Despite his challenges and failures, David made key decisions at strategic moments in his life that then paved the way for his success.

David started his journey as a young shepherd boy. In the darkness, he sat alone tending his father's sheep. In the quiet of the night, he could hear the call of greatness in his heart. David was the youngest of eight boys. He stayed at home doing the thankless task of sheepherding while his older brothers were off achieving glory in battle, so his life may have seemed like anything but great. Still, he heard the genuine calling of God.

You may also feel as though you have been left alone at home, but in your heart, you know that you too have heard

God's calling to greatness. He carved it into your DNA. You may have even heard it at a young age. Somehow you know God has called you to do something significant—to leave a mark on this world and make your life count for something. But if you are like most people, something happened along the way, and you feel hopelessly stuck.

Of course, all of us get distracted at times by obstacles such as money, fame, power, accomplishment, position, or beauty. The world measures greatness by those passing things. They don't actually define real greatness, though. When God set you into your mother's womb, He did it for something far greater than merely having the outward trappings that impress the world.

God created you to change people's lives. He called you for an eternal purpose as you worship and serve Him. Even though the world may be blind to their presence, truly great people surround you every day. These are the ones who have surrendered to the purpose God created them to carry out.

These people, such as King David, have not sold out to the cheap substitute of greatness that the world offers. They refuse the fleeting praise of the crowds so they can hear the only voice that matters say, "Well done, good and faithful servant…. Enter into the joy of your Master" (Matthew 25:23 ESV).

When I talk about truly great people who are largely overlooked by society, I am thinking of those who

- sacrifice to raise godly children in a corrupt culture
- defend the sanctity of life
- fight for traditional, biblical marriage as they also fight for the health their own
- reach out to the forgotten and vulnerable of society
- build the local church and humbly live the gospel before their friends, family, and neighbors

- take positions of leadership and influence in society and use those roles to advance the purposes of God regardless of the persecution they might endure
- use their wealth to advance God's Kingdom purposes
- refuse to lower their moral or personal standards below those of Scripture regardless of what temptations they may face or what society says about them

From the second you were born, your enemy has been working full-time to steer you away from greatness. However, let me tell you, *he will fail.* The apostle John says, "The one who is in you is greater than the one who is in the world" (1 John 4:4 NIV). The One who created you for greatness is stronger than the one who schemes to destroy you. The One who loves you and holds your future in His hands is mightier than the one who hates you and tries to bind you to the failures of your past. If I didn't believe this, I don't think I could believe anything else.

I love the story of King David because he is very much like the rest of us. You think you have made a mess of your life? Then meet David. *I am David, and so are you.* He has both strengths and weaknesses. Sometimes he slew giants; other times he committed great sins. Even so, there was never a time when God forsook or rejected David. Even through his failures, David never walked away from God, which is what made him a man after God's own heart and enabled him to fulfill God's call of greatness on his life. *Yes, I am David. You are David too.*

👑 **I am David, and so are you.**

So really, do you want to be great? If so, are you ready to walk away from the past and into the future God has planned for you? Are you willing to turn away from the voices of condemnation, shame, regret, insecurity, and fear that would try to drown out God's call of greatness in your heart of hearts?

Yes, you are ready?

Then let's follow King David's journey to greatness.

Part One

THE WARRIOR

JOIN THE BATTLE

OVER DECADES AS a pastor and counselor, I have encountered people from many different walks of life. Despite their economic or cultural differences, all of them had a hunger and a capacity for greatness. Wanting greatness and achieving it, however, are two very different matters. Societal forces work to suppress our desires for greatness, and Satan does his best to crush them. Even so, our hearts cry out for something more.

How can you discover your calling to greatness? How can you find the satisfaction of real achievement? I will tell you that until you do, you will experience persistent frustration. I want to help you move from simply having a desire for greatness to actually fulfilling that inborn drive God gave you. Here is the *first lesson,* and it begins with this simple truth about greatness: You won't discover your true greatness until you find it on the battlefield. And this truth has no exceptions.

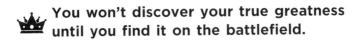 **You won't discover your true greatness until you find it on the battlefield.**

From the fall of humanity until the present day, every person ever born was wired for war. I don't necessarily mean for violence, but I do mean all of us must battle and struggle.

On the battlefield, we fulfill our calling and find greatness. Away from the battlefield, we find only frustration and failure, and then we forget who we are.

No person ever experienced the heights and depths of this fundamental truth more than Israel's King David. David's character, internal motives, and personal qualities didn't manifest themselves when the cameras started rolling. David wasn't an opportunist who waited for his moment when the crowds might be watching. No, greatness emerged in young David's life when only God was watching him herd his father's sheep. David became a warrior long before he went to war. He risked his life fighting the bear and the lion because he believed the price of even one lamb's life was too high. He applied that same thinking when King Saul questioned him before David confronted the giant Goliath:

> Your servant used to keep his father's sheep, and when a lion or a bear came and took a lamb out of the flock, I went out after it and struck it, and delivered *the lamb* from its mouth; and when it arose against me, I caught *it* by its beard, and struck and killed it. Your servant has killed both lion and bear; and this uncircumcised Philistine will be like one of them, seeing he has defied the armies of the living God.... The Lord, who delivered me from the paw of the lion and from the paw of the bear, He will deliver me from the hand of this Philistine (1 Samuel 17:34–37).

Yes, the stuff David was made of emerged long before he was in the public eye. He had *chosen the battlefield* even as he tended sheep. And when seasoned soldiers trembled and fell back in fear before Goliath, the champion who stepped forward was a young shepherd boy who had learned to trust God in anonymity while facing lions and bears.

THE STUFF HEROES ARE MADE OF

Some battles seem small and others large, yet David became a great warrior on the battlefield long ago as a young shepherd. He refused to be robbed by lions or bears because under God he had made a covenant to care for his father's property. In the same way, David trusted the Lord to keep His covenant. When David faced the uncircumcised Philistine giant who had openly challenged God's covenant nation, he knew the God of Israel would help him to prevail. David had the stuff real heroes are made of.

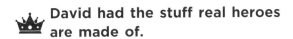 **David had the stuff real heroes are made of.**

Our culture today crowns heroes who help us enjoy our leisure time—movie stars, music idols, and standout athletes. But in David's time, the battlefield was the arena for selecting heroes. A shepherd boy who brought down the enemy's champion and delivered a nation had the crowds buzzing. The song of his victory over Goliath and the Philistines was the pop hit of the day. People danced in the streets to the catchy lyrics of "Saul has slain his thousands, And David his ten thousands" (1 Samuel 18:7 TLB).

The greatest years of David's life were those spent on the battlefield striking down the enemies of God. Today, we must recognize that not all the conflicts we face as warriors are taking place on the military front, but there are battles taking place on *every front* of our lives. In fact, the great Battle of the Ages is raging right now all around us. The biggest battle we face is for the lives and souls of our children, our spouses, our neighbors, and our friends. A Philistine giant is a small enemy in comparison. Our performance in *that* battle determines our true greatness because as we engage our enemy on the front, we then become truly great in God's eyes.

After the defeat of Goliath, David became greater and greater, and Israel's greatness grew as well. Do you still want greatness? If so, it's in the battle where you will reach your highest accomplishments. Your greatest successes will come through serving Jesus Christ and warring against the devil, not just for your own life but also for the lives of others. Without exception, the greatest years of your life will be those you spend on the battlefield serving the Lord.

MADE FOR THE BATTLEFIELD, NOT THE ROOFTOP

David's best years happened when he guarded what God had given him to protect and took back what the enemy had stolen. Nevertheless, even David was not always faithful. On one spring day, he made the fateful decision not to go into battle. It led to the worst choice of his life.

> It happened in the spring of the year, at the time when kings go out *to battle*, that David sent Joab and his servants with him, and all Israel; and they destroyed the people of Ammon and besieged Rabbah. But David remained at Jerusalem (2 Samuel 11:1).

On that particular day, David slid out of bed and took a stroll on the roof of his palace. He peered over the side to the houses below, and something caught his eye. A short distance away, a woman was bathing on her own rooftop. David likely recognized her since she was the spouse of one of his most trusted warriors. The biblical text says she was "very beautiful to behold" (2 Samuel 11:2). If only the story ended there, but sadly, it does not.

> David sent and inquired about the woman. And *someone* said, "*Is* this not Bathsheba, the daughter of Eliam, the wife of Uriah the Hittite?" Then David sent messengers, and took her; and she came to him, and he lay with her, for she was cleansed from her impurity; and she returned to her house. And the woman conceived; so she sent and told David, and said, "I *am* with child" (2 Samuel 11:3–5).

If this is the first time you have read this story, let it sink in for a minute. Israel's greatest king had a not-so-great moment. However, this story of David and Bathsheba doesn't really begin with David leering at another man's wife over the palace roof. On the contrary, it starts with David's uncharacteristic choice to stay home from the battle. This passage says it was "the time when kings go out to battle." David was a king, yet David was not going to battle. Something very wrong was happening. He was not a feeble old man. David was still young enough to participate actively in warfare, and his expected role was to lead his soldiers into battle. Yet he stayed home. David retired from battle.

The implications of this decision stretched far beyond the obvious complications of an adulterous affair and an unexpected pregnancy. David's decision to stay home instead of engaging in battle marked the beginning of the end of greatness in his kingship *and* his life. From this point on, his story is filled with dysfunction and destruction for both himself and his family.

URIAH, FAITHFUL IN BATTLE

David followed up his initial bad decision with more bad decisions. Once he discovered Bathsheba's pregnancy, he panicked and tried to cover up the affair. Desperately hoping to make it appear that her husband, Uriah, was the father of the baby, David summoned the soldier from the battle-front and enticed him to go home to sleep with his wife (see 2 Samuel 11:6–8). If he could accomplish this ruse, David reasoned that no one would be the wiser.

This plan, however, came with one fatal flaw in reasoning: Uriah knew where he belonged. Uriah would not consent to having intimate relations with his wife while his fellow soldiers were still sleeping on the battlefield. David discovered Uriah's refusal and asked him why he had slept on the palace porch instead of returning home to his wife. Uriah answered him with a question: "How can I sleep with my wife and enjoy the benefits of my home when my fellow soldiers are on the battlefield?" (see verse 11). The unspoken implications of this question were far-reaching. How could *David* enjoy the comforts of his home, let alone the comforts of another man's wife, while his men were fighting and dying in battle?

Uriah proved himself a man of honor. His commitment to duty forced David's hand; the king would attempt another ploy to cover up his crime. So David arranged to party with Uriah, thinking that what Uriah would not do sober, he might do under the influence of alcohol. But even drunk, this honorable warrior would not enjoy the comfort of his wife's bed, at least not while knowing his fellow soldiers were sleeping in tents on the battlefront.

David's panic only grew as he urgently tried to cover Bathsheba's pregnancy—which, don't forget, was a result of his shirking his military responsibilities. The king then devised his most sinister deception. He ordered Uriah back to the field of action. Unknowingly, this devoted soldier carried his own death sentence in the form of a note from the king to the commander. David's note gave instructions for Uriah to be sent into the heat of the battle and then for the rest of the troops to pull back from him so the enemy would certainly kill him. This plan was bad enough, but David also miscalculated the honor of his own soldiers. Many of them died at the hands of the enemy that day because they refused to retreat and leave Uriah all alone. The deadliness of David's sin was real—and growing.

When the report of Uriah's death came, David supposed his cover up was a success. However, David failed to take account of someone who knew about every detail: God. And God sent His prophet, Nathan, to expose the whole sordid mess:

> Then the LORD sent Nathan to David. And he came to him, and said to him: "There were two men in one city, one rich and the other poor. The rich *man* had exceedingly many flocks and herds. But the poor *man* had nothing, except one little ewe lamb which he had bought and nourished; and it grew up together with him and with his children. It ate of his own food and drank from his own cup and lay in his bosom; and it was like a daughter to him. And a traveler came to the rich man, who refused to take from his own flock and from his own herd to prepare one for the wayfaring man who had come to him; but he took the poor man's lamb and prepared it for the man who had come to him."
>
> So David's anger was greatly aroused against the man, and he said to Nathan, "*As* the LORD lives, the man who has done this shall surely die! And he shall restore fourfold for the lamb, because he did this thing and because he had no pity."

Then Nathan said to David, "You *are* the man! Thus says the Lord God of Israel: 'I anointed you king over Israel, and I delivered you from the hand of Saul. I gave you your master's house and your master's wives into your keeping, and gave you the house of Israel and Judah. And if *that had been* too little, I also would have given you much more! Why have you despised the command-ment of the Lord, to do evil in His sight? You have killed Uriah the Hittite with the sword; you have taken his wife *to be* your wife, and have killed him with the sword of the people of Ammon. Now therefore, the sword shall never depart from your house, because you have despised Me, and have taken the wife of Uriah the Hittite to be your wife.' Thus says the Lord: 'Behold, I will raise up adversity against you from your own house; and I will take your wives before your eyes and give *them* to your neighbor, and he shall lie with your wives in the sight of this sun. For you did *it* secretly, but I will do this thing before all Israel, before the sun.' "

So David said to Nathan, "I have sinned against the Lord."

And Nathan said to David, "The Lord also has put away your sin; you shall not die. However, because by this deed you have given great occasion to the enemies of the Lord to blaspheme, the child also *who is* born to you shall surely die." Then Nathan departed to his house (2 Samuel 12:1–15).

I include this entire passage to show you what God did with David. David decided he would make his own choices, including the decision not to go to battle. God allowed him to continue making his own choices, although David did not even realize it. David declared, "*As* the Lord lives, the man who has done this shall surely die! And he shall restore fourfold for the lamb, because he did this thing and because he had no pity" (vv. 5–6). Little did he know, but David was pronouncing his own judgment. God spared his life, but four of his children ("fourfold") would die as a result of David's sin. The cost was high.

King David was great on the battlefield but corrupt on the rooftop. So why, in this particular year, when it was time to go to battle, did David, the skilled warrior and leader, decide not to go to war? The answer to that question will reveal the common pitfalls we all experience on the road to greatness. It will help us understand why some of us do not go into the war zone—and ultimately why we never achieve greatness.

THE 3 LIES OF RETREAT

God created you to be great and to *finish* great. No wonder the enemy spends massive amounts of time trying to keep you from discovering who you really are. It's also no surprise he worked so hard to bring down Israel's mightiest king. David was a great man, and we can discover a lot from his rise to greatness, but what we learn from his fall is equally important. Why, after many years as a great military leader with legendary success on the battlefield, did David choose to remain home? He started believing lies. These same lies are common in our day, and they caused him to make his decision. *Three lies*, in particular, will keep you from finishing great.

> God created you to be great and to *finish* great.

23

LIE #1: YOU'VE EARNED THE "RIGHT" TO RETIRE

Is it possible for a warrior to reach a level of success so great that he or she no longer has the duty to fight or work? Perhaps David believed that once he had established a successful kingship, he no longer needed to fight and had earned the right to stay home.

Many Americans, including Christians, buy into this kind of thinking. Many young adults consider early retirement as their loftiest goal. Older adults fear the inability to retire comfortably. What is "the American Dream"? Many in the US would define it as having enough resources to sit in a lounge chair on a beautiful beach while sipping an umbrella cocktail. Television ads and infomercials hawk this version of "success." The lengthy ads promise products that will help us gain financial independence with little or no responsibility for anything else. They are selling a philosophy that truly successful individuals arrive at a state of total financial independence, taking orders from no one and avoiding anyone else unless you want to encounter them on your own terms.

What could be wrong with this goal, besides the statistical improbability of it? Nowhere do the Scriptures contain the concept of "retirement." The Bible also never even hints that we will reach a time in our lives when we shouldn't actively be serving the Lord. As believers, we are on the battlefield. We win people to Christ. We serve in church. We do what God has called us to do, and we serve Him until we take our final breath.

Of course, the *way* we work or war may change. You may reach a point in your life when you can no longer perform manual labor or respond to other physical demands in the same way you did when you were younger. You may even reach the place financially where you no longer need structured employment. Yes, your job may change, and you may have more money in the bank. Even so, none of that will give you the "right" to leave the battlefield and stop serving the Lord. He commissioned you to serve until the day you die.

Both Pope John Paul II and Billy Graham lived out this truth. If anyone had earned the right to retire, these men did. But *did* either one of them retire? No! While I am not a Roman Catholic, I admire Pope John Paul II. For many years before his death in 2005, he was extremely frail, yet he didn't stop traveling the world. He worked every day, all day. When he couldn't stand on his own, his aides physically propped him up. They held a microphone in front of him so he could continue his duties. He served God until the moment he died. Billy Graham also exemplified staying on the battlefield until the end of his life. The last time I saw him preaching, though he was dealing with deafness and Parkinson's disease, I said to myself, *That is the way I'm going to be!* He was an inspiration to all of us who serve the Lord. He is only the fourth private citizen, and the only religious leader, ever to lie in state in the United States Capitol rotunda.

I want to preach for the rest of my life. Thirty years from now, if Jesus tarries and I'm still around in my 90s, I'll know more than I know today. I'll be wiser than I am today. I might not be as energetic, but just prop me up and give me a microphone, and I'll preach! My wife, Karen, and I don't have plans that include retirement. Why would we? When does God ever say that we can abandon our post on the battlefield?

God never set the age of 65 as a cut-off point for doing the work to which He has called us. The federal government originally set that age for receiving full Social Security benefits. You may draw Social Security when you reach a certain age, but that does not mean you can withdraw from serving God. Many people over 65 serve God with all of their hearts, while some in their 20s and 30s have not yet joined the battle. Retirement is not an age issue—it is an attitude issue.

Likewise, when David retired from the battlefield, it was an attitude issue. He wasn't too old to go to war, but he may have thought that he had enough gold and silver saved up and he could retire with few responsibilities. Perhaps he had so much luxury around him that he said to himself, *I've got everything I need! I don't need to go back to the battlefield.*

The choice to remain in the palace started David down the road toward the end of his greatness. Think about all the amazing times he spent serving God and the nation of Israel. When David decided to stay home from battle, the bad years began.

Created to Defeat an Archenemy

When God created human beings, He knew the devil and demons were already present in the universe. Adam and Eve may not have realized it, but God knew they were in a war zone. His mandate to Adam included the words "subdue" and "take dominion"—violent words. Today, we face the same battle. No matter where you go in your life, it's a battlefield. Be aware that God wired you for war, because you are right in the middle of one—and it is not going to go away.

However, the battle is not the end of the story. The apostle Paul tells us that not only are we are made for battle, but we are also given the tools to win:

> My brethren, be strong in the Lord and in the power of His might. Put on the whole armor of God, that you may be able to stand against the wiles of the devil. For we do not wrestle against flesh and blood, but against principalities, against powers, against the rulers of the darkness of this age, against spiritual *hosts* of wickedness in the heavenly

places. Therefore take up the whole armor of God, that you may be able to withstand in the evil day, and having done all, to stand (Ephesians 6:10–13).

Your enemy is stalking you. He's all around you looking for an opportunity. That is why you must put on the full armor of God and leave it on every moment of every day.

Yes, God has given you authority over the enemy, but that authority isn't worth a rusty penny if you don't use it. All the authority in the world couldn't save King David from the corruption of rooftop thinking and a rooftop lifestyle. The rooftop is a place of darkness, where people try to escape from God's will for their lives. Just as the battlefield creates good men and women, so also the rooftop robs them of greatness. No one can avoid the negative consequences of refusing to fight.

Perhaps you've been serving God and have become tired. Maybe you think you've earned the right to take a vacation from your normal schedule and—to some extent—from God. Well, if you think lowering your standards for just a little bit while you are away won't hurt anything, think again! It surely will do some damage. A vacation from God is a vacation with the devil, and the devil doesn't play nice. And when you come back from a vacation with the devil, it takes months, if not years, to recover.

Turning from battle, even for a moment, is not an option. Too much is at stake. Leaving your post affects not only you but also your friends, family, marriage, and children. Goliath's taunts were a threat not just to the man who would dare face him, but they were also threats to the families of every soldier on the field that day. If Goliath had won, all the families of Israel would have become slaves to the Philistines.

No less is at stake today. When the devil takes us down, our children fall. Communities fall too. For that reason, there is no such thing as "private sin." If we stand and fight, many people go free. If we give in to the deception of the rooftop, others will be taken captive with us.

David's sin affected his family in a dramatic way for generations. The best times in David's life—the most peaceful, restful, enjoyable, glorious, bountiful times—were the years on the battlefield. The secret of peace is not resting on the rooftop. It is winning on the battlefield.

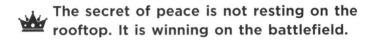

The secret of peace is not resting on the rooftop. It is winning on the battlefield.

LIE #2: YOU CAN HIDE PREMEDITATED SIN

Another reason why David stayed home might have been that he'd already spotted Bathsheba and was waiting for an opportunity to approach her. Think about it: Bathsheba was bathing naked on her rooftop, which was obviously close to David's house. We can surmise that proximity because even though he had no binoculars to assist him in plotting his sin, he had no trouble seeing her from his rooftop. It may have been that Bathsheba could see him as well and was aware that he was watching her. She may not fully share David's guilt, but she certainly knew where to take a bath.

My guess is that the occasion leading immediately to David's adultery with Bathsheba was not the first time he had seen her. I also suspect she was aware all along that he had been watching her. Her bathing time may, in fact, have become a regular if unspoken appointment for her to display herself to him. And so that year, when it came time for all the kings and their forces to engage in battle, David had another plan. He was waiting for Uriah to leave town so he could send for Bathsheba and have sex with her.

The theory that David stayed home because of a premeditated decision can't be proven with certainty. One thing, however, *is* certain: that one act of adultery with Bathsheba caused David more pain than any war he had ever fought. What no lion, bear, giant, enemy army, or jealous king could do, a single night of sin did to David. It caused him pain for the rest of his life and extended beyond his life.

Premeditated sin keeps many people out of the battle. If the devil can't kill you with a bullet, he'll try using a Bathsheba. Many people today are not on the battlefield because they are on a rooftop. That rooftop may be pornography or other illicit materials. Or it may be some other sin. But they have chosen to pursue that sin instead of participating in the battle.

When I was 19 years old, I was an immoral, ungodly young man. I had spent years partying hard, and I liked it. A week before Karen and I were to marry, I was involved in a series of very bad things. What I did was so bad that Karen told me she wouldn't marry me. Thankfully, that situation led me to the point of a decision to accept Jesus as my Savior and serve Him the rest of my life.

The day I received the Lord, I thought, *If I serve the Lord, it will be like signing up for boot camp for the rest of my life. Pleasure will no longer be part of my life. The rest of my life is not going to be about enjoying myself. Serving God means giving up everything I enjoy.*

When I made my decision to accept the Lord in my life, I made it with that false evaluation in mind. But I want you to know that just the opposite has been true. Sin would have killed me, and serving God has been more enjoyable than I could ever have imagined.

Romans 6:23 tells us, "The wages of sin *is* death." That truth has never been altered. The devil will promise you a life of leisure and rest—then he will hack your heart out. God promises you a life of battle, and then He gives you a life of blessing and increase.

Every person who desires to be great and finish great needs to understand this: the devil knows your price. He understands your vulnerabilities. David's vulnerability was a sexual problem. He took another man's wife even though his own house was filled with many wives and concubines. Likewise, Satan will hammer on you in the areas where you are weak to get you off the battlefield.

On the rooftop, you can be defeated. But on the field of battle, the enemy knows he is already defeated. On the battlefield, you and I are devil killers—champions waiting for a place to happen. On the battlefield, God forges our character, and we become the great men and women He created us to be.

LIE #3: YOU CAN'T KEEP WINNING

Another reason David stayed home from battle may be that he lost his nerve. Consider David's reputation as a warrior. I can imagine every enemy soldier on the battlefield would have considered killing or capturing David as a great trophy. With each new season of battle, the number of those who wanted to take down the renowned giant killer grew. All the young enemy soldiers knew taking down David would lead to overnight glory and fame. Remember, David wasn't getting any younger or stronger. Consequently, fear might have entered his heart as he considered his future on the battlefield. And fear keeps many warriors off the battlefield. I know this because it almost kept me out of the pulpit.

When the Lord called me to preach, I had a tremendous fear of public speaking—a fear so bad that it was demonic. The first time I was scheduled to teach in a home Bible study group, I was so terrified that I couldn't sleep for a week prior.

Then, when the time came, I started hyperventilating. On another occasion, I taught in one of the home groups in our church. The first man to walk out the door looked me in the eye and said, "You can't teach." This comment only reinforced my fear. So before I could pastor a large church and start a television ministry, I had to face my fear of public speaking and numerous other fears.

Can I tell you something personal? I still have fears. We all do, but we have to face them! Courage is not defined by how few fears a person has. Courage is a commitment to do the right thing *in spite* of fear. As Mark Twain said, "Courage is resistance to fear of fear; mastery of fear—not the absence of it."

♔ Courage is a commitment to do the right thing *in spite* of fear.

Good soldiers will keep advancing in spite of voices inside telling them to run away like scared children. The soldier stands and says, "I'm going to fight because it's right. I'm going to fight because my family is behind me, and if I give up, the enemy's going to get them. I'm going to fight because the souls of men and women depend on me, and God has called me to this battle."

Every born-again believer has that kind of courage residing inside, and every believer must call upon that courage in the day of battle. So, should you find yourself on the rooftop, stir up your courage, climb down from it, and return to the battlefield.

God's Word says that if you will submit to Him and resist the devil, then the devil will (not *might*) flee from you (James 4:7). It also says that if you will confess your sins to God, He is faithful and just to forgive you of those sins, and the blood of Jesus will cleanse you from all unrighteousness (see 1 John 1:9).

Just as the devil has a plan to pull you off the battlefield and into the downward spiral of sin and defeat, so also God has a plan to get you back into the fight so you can begin living a life that is rooftop-resistant and devil-destroying.

THE BATTLE IN YOUR HEAD

Jesus' crucifixion took place on a hill called Golgotha. That odd-sounding name means "the place of the skull." I have seen that hill, and it truly looks like a skull. That imagery is no coincidence. As the blood poured from Christ's body onto the ground, it dripped over that image of a human skull. Jesus came to give us life; He said, "I am the way, the truth, and the life" (John 14:6). He had to die and triumph over death, hell, and the grave to set our minds free so we could receive the truth and walk in that life.

No area of our lives can be set free until our minds are first set free in that area. Therefore, the first battle any great warrior must win is the battle for his or her own thoughts. Winning in this arena takes far greater courage than the bravery displayed in a military confrontation. It is in the battlefield of the mind that warriors make their first stand. There they take authority over the fears screaming inside their minds that encourage them to run from the fight. And if warriors find themselves in sin on a rooftop, it is in their will and mind that they must repent, overcome the shame, and return to the battlefield.

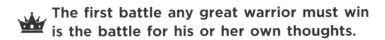 **The first battle any great warrior must win is the battle for his or her own thoughts.**

BREAKING THE CYCLE OF REPETITIVE SIN

No one is exempt from the temptations of worldliness, independence, and a desire to retire to a life of leisure. Among other things, every person is tempted with lust. Everyone also deals with fear. I believe all of us can relate to the reality of temptations that come to our minds. As warriors, what should we *do* when those temptations arise?

Obviously, we don't want to follow David's example from the rooftop. He chose the wrong course of action. David ended up in the wrong place at the wrong time because he lost the battle over his thoughts. The location opened the door for temptation, and his decision to give in to temptation cost him dearly.

Today, we all face the same kinds of challenges. One of the greatest temptations in our present culture is sexual sin. When surveyed, 53 percent of men who attended Promise Keepers said they viewed pornography that week. In an online newsletter, 34 percent of female readers of *Today's Christian Woman* admitted to accessing Internet pornography intentionally. The Internet fuels the problem by providing easy access to pornography and affording its viewers—both men and women—anonymity.

As with David, the location problem for people today precedes the sin problem. We are not *where* we should be if we are watching pornography. We are in the wrong location. We are destined to be in the battle fighting for our marriages, our families, and our relationship as children of God.

People who are looking at pornography may be putting up a good front by pretending to fulfill their calling. They may talk the talk and look the part. David did. He wore a king's robe and thought he could hide behind the pretense of carrying out his kingly duties. But God knew, and eventually He called David to account. There are many ways for us to play the game on the outside and make it appear that we are being warriors. But self-righteous pretense won't make the cut spiritually.

We must acknowledge that if a man like David can fall, any one of us can fall too. Not one of us is immune. We must be honest and recognize where we really belong—and stay in that place.

Now, if you are presently participating in repetitive sin, you may be thinking, *Well, I am trying to stop.* That may be true. But your success will be limited and temporary until you begin to rise up and take authority over what you're allowing into your thought life. You will never stop looking at pornography, stop drinking, or walk free of any sin or addiction until you war for your thoughts.

Second Corinthians 10:3–6 says,

> Though we walk in the flesh, we do not war according to the flesh. For the weapons of our warfare *are* not carnal but mighty in God for pulling down strongholds, casting down arguments and every high thing that exalts itself against the knowledge of God, bringing every thought into captivity to the obedience of Christ, and being ready to punish all disobedience when your obedience is fulfilled.

You don't belong on the rooftop looking at pornography. As a warrior, you have no business lusting after another person's wife or husband or someone who isn't your spouse. Where you do belong is on the battlefield—pulling down strongholds, casting down arguments, and bringing thoughts into captivity.

THE POWER OF TRUTH

The devil did not capture the human race with a bomb, a bullet, or a bazooka. In Genesis 3, he brought humankind down with a lie. In Matthew 4 and Luke 4, Jesus fights the battle of the universe in the wilderness. The devil squared off against Him by quoting half-Scripture against Scripture, half-truth against truth. But Jesus defeated him with the full and uncompromised Word of God. The battle was—and still is—a battle for truth. It's a battle that is first waged in our minds

The apostle Paul's instructions for preparing for the battle-field are found in Ephesians 6:13–17:

> Take up the whole armor of God, that you may be able to withstand in the evil day, and having done all, to stand.
>
> Stand therefore, having girded your waist with truth, having put on the breastplate of righteousness, and having shod your feet with the preparation of the gospel of peace; above all, taking the shield of faith with which you will be able to quench all the fiery darts of the wicked one. And take the helmet of salvation, and the sword of the Spirit, which is the word of God.

Paul wanted to equip us for a daily battle when he wrote these words. We win by putting on the whole armor of God. We win by recognizing the strategy of the enemy and suiting up with our armor against him. We win by taking up our position.

Try this: Wake up each morning and say, "I know the devil is going to war for my mind today. I know he's going to try to use images on billboards, magazines, the Internet, and television to tempt me. But I'm not giving my thoughts to him. I'm staying on the battlefield all day and all night."

As you roll over in bed at night, you have to war for your thoughts. When you wake up in the morning, you also have to war for your thoughts. It does not matter where you are or what we are doing. What matters is never forgetting that you have an evil enemy you can defeat if you will fight. But you can fight him only on the battlefield. The instant you withdraw from the battlefield, you give him entrance into your life. Just as giving the devil an entrance to his mind was the beginning of the end for King David, so following his example will be the beginning of the end for you and me.

On the battlefield, dressed in the full armor of God, you are unstoppable. You can put on the helmet of salvation and say, "I am going to fight a war for my thoughts. I am not giving my thoughts over to the devil." You wield the sword of the Spirit, which is the Word of God. That means saying what God says about your situation. You gird your loins—the area of reproduction and elimination—with truth. Girded with the armor of truth, you eliminate error and reproduce truth. Without that armor, you will reproduce error and eliminate truth.

WHERE CAN WE FIND PEOPLE OF GREATNESS?

As I said previously, our culture tends to make heroes out of people who pamper our desires for leisure. It esteems those who are living what is perceived of as "the American Dream." We are accustomed to hearing people sing the praises of someone who is a great businessperson, a great performer, a great athlete, and so on.

In reality, greatness has little to do with fame or how much money a person has earned, No one is truly great who doesn't serve Jesus Christ. True greatness has everything to do with how many souls we take with us to heaven and how honorably we serve the Lord Jesus Christ, not only in front of people but also behind the scenes.

 No one is truly great who doesn't serve Jesus Christ.

When bombarded by everything from lustful pictures to fear-inducing images of world terrorism, the truly great person—the man or woman of God—will say, "I will not withdraw from the battlefield. It's where I belong." In the same way, a person made for greatness who is caught on the rooftop will have the courage to admit, "I have withdrawn from the front lines," and then declare, "Right now I turn around and go back to the battlefront. I realize my greatest experiences and my quickest growth have always been those years in the battle. My worst years have been on the rooftop. The devil made it seem good, but it has only produced torment. I am made for battle. I am equipped for battle. And battle is the only place I know where I can win."

I should warn you of something you already know: the only people you will find on the rooftop are other rooftop people. They are those who are willing to sin and then do anything in their power to cover it up. You will never become great around rooftop people. If you realize the kind of people with whom you are associating are of the rooftop variety, break off your close connection to them! Do an about-face and go the other way. Go to the battlefield and find fellow warriors. You'll become great by being with great people. When you find a person who has chosen to fight and win the battle over his or her thought life, you have found someone on the pathway to destiny. This person is a fellow warrior who will cover your back. That is the kind of person you want to have as a friend. This is not to say the people you find on the battlefield have never made mistakes. Everyone makes mistakes, which brings me to the next chapter and the second lesson about every great person.

TAKE RESPONSIBILITY FOR YOUR MISTAKES

WHEN YOU GET away from rooftop people and start surrounding yourself with real warriors who are on the road to greatness, you will quickly realize that even great warriors are not perfect. It is then you will discover the second truth about greatness: every great person takes responsibility for his or her mistakes and becomes greater through them.

You may have even made some terrible mistakes. Perhaps you've committed adultery. Or you have an addiction to pornography. You may have compromised yourself in your work. You know you've violated basic Christian ethics. You might have stolen something. Or you've participated some way in an abortion. The possible list is too long even for a book. Well, if you've done any of these things or others, know that you are not alone—*everyone* makes mistakes.

Your mistakes are not what will keep you from attaining the greatness for which God has destined you. What determines whether you become a true champion or not is what you *do* about those mistakes. In fact, taking responsibility is what makes the difference between failure and success. Someone who takes responsibility for his or her own mistakes is a person of greatness.

👑 **Taking responsibility is what makes the difference between failure and success.**

The Bible begins with people who fail to take responsibility for their mistakes. In Genesis 3, Adam and Eve disobey God in the Garden of Eden. Then God asks Adam, "What is this that you've done?" Instead of taking responsibility for his own actions, Adam points the finger at Eve and said, "It's her fault." In response to the same question from God, Eve blames the serpent. Like her husband, she tries to duck responsibility. Throughout the ages, people have followed this same destructive pattern. Multitudes have blamed their problems on their wives or husbands, their moms or dads, and their bosses or coworkers. They will point their fingers at everyone but themselves.

Jesus had the opposite response. He was a real man who took responsibility for Himself and others around Him. Jesus knew no sin, yet He willingly let Himself take on the responsibility of sin for us so we could be made right with God (2 Corinthians 5:21). He took our deserved punishment for sin!

Consider the amazing fact that when Jesus was crucified, He wanted to make sure His mother's future was secure. As he hung on the cross and looked down at His mother, He said, "Woman, behold your son!" He looked at the apostle John and said, "Behold your mother!" (John 19:26–27). Jesus was telling John that His mother was now in John's care going forward.

What a great man! What a great example Jesus set for us!

GREAT PEOPLE TELL

David committed some terrible mistakes in his life. I can certainly relate to that. I, too, have made some really bad mistakes. One thing I love about David is that he never gave up, and at the greatest failure in his life, he took responsibility for his sins.

The title over Psalm 51 reads: "A Psalm of David when Nathan the prophet went to him after he had gone in to Bathsheba." David wrote this song after Nathan the prophet had confronted him with God's message about his sin, saying in effect, "David, you have taken another man's wife and slept with her, and you killed that man." Although he made some terrible mistakes, this response shows why David became known as "a man after God's own heart."

Out of brokenness for his sin, David wrote:

Have mercy upon me, O God,
According to Your lovingkindness;
According to the multitude of Your tender mercies,
Blot out my transgressions.
Wash me thoroughly from my iniquity,
And cleanse me from my sin.
For I acknowledge my transgressions,
And my sin *is* always before me.
Against You, You only, have I sinned,
And done *this* evil in Your sight (Psalm 51:1–4).

Notice that David *didn't* say, "I have sinned against Bathsheba, I sinned against Uriah, and I sinned against my wives and concubines." He said, "Lord, I have sinned against You. This is about me and You, God. This isn't about me and another person. Against You, You only, have I sinned, and done this evil in your sight."

David didn't make an attempt to justify his behavior. He didn't try to minimize it. He didn't say, "Well, I had this little problem with lust." He admitted what he had done was *evil*. David was willing to tell the truth.

He didn't point his finger at his wife Abigail and say, "She's just not meeting my needs." He didn't blame Bathsheba and say, "Well, she's just really pretty. Who could resist that?" He didn't accuse God and say, "You made me with these desires. What am I supposed to do about them?"

No. David didn't denounce anybody else. He pointed his finger straight at himself and said, "I've done an evil thing. I've sinned against You, Lord. And I pray that You would forgive me and create in me a clean heart."

> Against You, You only, have I sinned,
> And done this evil in Your sight—
> That You may be found just when You speak,
> And blameless when You judge.
> Behold, I was brought forth in iniquity,
> And in sin my mother conceived me.
> Behold, You desire truth in the inward parts,
> And in the hidden part You will make me to know wisdom.
> Purge me with hyssop, and I shall be clean;
> Wash me, and I shall be whiter than snow.
> Make me hear joy and gladness,
> That the bones You have broken may rejoice.
> Hide Your face from my sins,
> And blot out all my iniquities.
> Create in me a clean heart, O God,
> And renew a steadfast spirit within me.
> Do not cast me away from Your presence,
> And do not take Your Holy Spirit from me.
> Restore to me the joy of Your salvation,
> And uphold me by Your generous Spirit.
> Then I will teach transgressors Your ways,
> And sinners shall be converted to You.
> Deliver me from the guilt of bloodshed, O God,
> The God of my salvation,

And my tongue shall sing aloud of Your righteousness.
O Lord, open my lips,
And my mouth shall show forth Your praise.
For You do not desire sacrifice, or else I would give it;
You do not delight in burnt offering.
The sacrifices of God are a broken spirit,
A broken and a contrite heart—
These, O God, You will not despise.
Do good in Your good pleasure to Zion;
Build the walls of Jerusalem.
Then You shall be pleased with the sacrifices of
righteousness,
With burnt offering and whole burnt offering;
Then they shall offer bulls on Your altar (Psalm 51:4–19).

A BAD SINNER, BUT A GREAT REPENTER

David was a bad sinner, but he was also a great repenter.
He didn't run from God in his sin. Instead, David ran *to*
God. And God forgave and restored him! He didn't reject
David. God doesn't throw people away; rather, He is into
redeeming them. Why? Because people who have done some
really bad things and made really bad mistakes have the
ability to become great, and God alone sees that wonderful
possibility.

That is why, without qualification, I can say to you: *you
are a warrior at heart.* God created you for that and it is who
you are. He made you to be a devil killer. When God formed
you in your mother's womb, it was for a purpose higher than
anything you can comprehend. He created you to snatch
people out of the kingdom of darkness by telling them about
the kingdom of heaven. God made you to bring the message of
salvation and hope to people living in your community. You

have an anointing straight from God to deliver people whom the devil is oppressing.

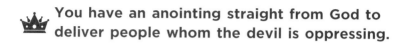 **You have an anointing straight from God to deliver people whom the devil is oppressing.**

Your purpose in life is not to earn money. It's not to become comfortable. You were not created just to have all the trinkets around you that the world says make you important. It's about helping other people and serving your Savior and Commander-in-Chief. That's what makes you great in God's sight.

Greatness comes from going onto the battlefield and facing the enemy. It is about being a warrior in spite of temptation, in spite of lust, in spite of the fear the devil plants in your heart. It's about standing your ground.

Since you are a warrior at heart, you can choose to die in battle with your boots on rather than die on the rooftop wearing a silk robe and taking something that doesn't belong to you. If your life ends in the midst of pursuing your dream, at least you will die while serving Jesus. That would be an honorable death.

David suffered terrible consequences for his decision to turn away from the battle. But he was a great repenter, and when he took responsibility for his actions, God heard his cry.

GOD HASN'T GIVEN UP ON YOU

What I want you to realize is God has not given up on you. Regardless of what you've done, how you've failed, or where you are at this moment, I want you to *know* that God hasn't changed His intention for your life. He's destined you for greatness and has a plan that will take you into that destiny.

If you have a problem with pornography, fantasy lust, adultery, or any other issues, you can wrestle with that sin all you want, but it will never go away until you get on the battlefield where your true greatness can be developed. Just say before God, "I am enlisting in Your service. I am going to war for my thoughts. I am going to war for my future. I am going to war for my family. And I am going to war for people who may not even know me. But because You care about them, and because my life can make a difference in their lives, I will fight for them, too." If you have an issue in your life, then you need to deal with and be honest about it. Shame is the devil's tool. We all make mistakes. We have an evil enemy that's on our case, dogging us to step over into sin.

David is an example of a person who made a great mistake but then owned up to it. God forgave him. Then God placed David's confession and God's forgiveness at a prominent place in the Bible for us to see. The Lord wanted to encourage us and show us the way to receive His mercy and grace. Psalm 51 is a beautiful picture of a person who truly came to God with a repentant heart and then received God's forgiveness. David doesn't point his finger. There's no minimizing or justifying it. David simply took ownership of it and said, "God, I've sinned, and I repent."

What was David's mistake? Being on the rooftop? No, the mistake was *not* being on the battlefield. What happened on the rooftop was borne out of his absence from the battlefield.

What did God do about it? He forgave.

Forgiveness is what God is offering you right now. Don't try to hide your sin—confess it! To confess your sin to God means you agree with Him that it has no part in your life and you want to turn away from it forever. The Bible says, "Confess *your* trespasses to one another, and pray for one another, that you may be healed. The effective, fervent prayer of a righteous man avails much" (James 5:16). Forgiveness is available to you. Healing is available to you. Greatness is available to you. Will you receive it?

 Forgiveness is available to you. Healing is available to you. Greatness is available to you.

The Warrior's Prayer

Lord, we are warriors. We are engaged in a battle—a fight against principalities, against powers, against the rulers of the darkness of this age, and against spiritual hosts of wickedness in the heavenly places.

Our children are under attack. Our marriages are under attack. Our public schools are under attack. Our communities are under attack. Everything sacred on this earth is under attack. We're locked in a battle.

But Jesus, You said that You give us all authority in heaven and on earth. You give us authority to bind and loose, to trample upon serpents and scorpions and over all the power of the enemy. You give us power to rule our minds righteously, to rule our bodies and not to give them over to the lusts of the flesh. You give us authority over our fears, because You haven't given us the spirit of fear but of love and of power and of a sound mind.

I know You have created me for greatness and given me the authority to make a difference on the earth. Give me the strength of conviction to fight harder and be a faithful soldier for You on the battlefield. And to whatever extent I have found myself on the rooftop instead of the battlefield, I repent. The rooftop can promise me only the worst years of my life. I will spend my best years on the battlefield serving You and doing Your will, just as did King David. Father, I willingly enlist in Your service. I lay down whatever has kept me off the battlefield. Any lure of money

---

or desire for success that is pulling me away from what You created me to be and do, I lay it down. All excuses of busyness for the sake of my career, every sin, every fear of failure—whatever I have used to justify continuing not to serve You—I lay it down right now.

From this day forward, I choose to be a great person—a person who chooses the battlefield and service to Jesus, my Commander-in-Chief. I choose to be a person of honor and duty, a warrior like Uriah the Hittite and like David before he fell.

Father, deliver me from every bondage and fear. Anoint me to be a warrior who fights for those who cannot fight for themselves and claim the victory You already won for us over our enemy, the devil. Touch my hands, my mind, and my mouth with the anointing of Jesus Christ.

In Jesus' name I pray, Amen.

Part Two

THE WOUNDED SON

RISE ABOVE THE PAIN OF THE PAST

I HAVE ALREADY revealed two of the ten lessons about greatness: every great person becomes great on the battlefield, and every great person takes responsibility for his or her mistakes. Now, I want you to consider another truth. Every person has been hurt in some way or another, and the third truth about greatness is this: every great person rises above the pain of the past to reach his or her God-given destiny.

In this chapter, I will discuss something you may not hear much about—the years David suffered pain as a result of rejection from his father, his eldest brother, and King Saul. That pain produced a pattern in his life that is also gnawing at the heart of many men and women today. That pattern is one of suffering silently while our family units disintegrate.

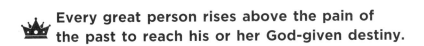 **Every great person rises above the pain of the past to reach his or her God-given destiny.**

IGNORED BY HIS DAD

David was a man of vast contrasts. For example, the Bible describes a wide difference between David, the successful military leader and David, the failed husband and father. This fact raises an obvious question: with such great strengths as a military leader, why was David so weak as a parent? To answer that question, consider the events surrounding his anointing as king. In 1 Samuel, we discover David was the youngest of eight brothers. The Bible text also doesn't show that David received much attention from his own father.

At the time of David's anointing, Saul was king of Israel. King Saul was a man of tremendous potential, but he only made a halfhearted commitment to God's leadership. Eventually, his failure to repent of his rebellion caused God to reject him as king. The Lord instructed the prophet Samuel to go to the house of a man named Jesse and anoint a new king of Israel. It is of great significance that the Jesse only introduced seven of his sons to Samuel—remember, he had *eight* sons! David, the youngest, was left in the field to tend sheep. First Samuel 16:10–11 says,

> Jesse made seven of his sons pass before Samuel. And Samuel said to Jesse, "The Lord has not chosen these." And Samuel said to Jesse, "Are all the young men here?" Then he said, "There remains yet the youngest, and there he is, keeping the sheep."

What must have been going on in David's heart? Every one of us has felt what David probably did that day. David must have been within viewing distance of all of the ceremony and excitement going on with the rest of his family. He was close enough that when Samuel rejected his brothers and asked if there was not another son to consider, David's dad was able to point him out to Samuel. And then what happened?

> Samuel said to Jesse, "Send and bring him. For we will not sit down till he comes here." So he sent and brought him

in. Now he *was* ruddy, with bright eyes, and good-looking. And the Lord said, "Arise, anoint him; for this *is* the one!" Then Samuel took the horn of oil and anointed him in the midst of his brothers; and the spirit of the Lord came upon David from that day forward (vv. 11–13).

Consider for a moment this situation. How devastating was it to be the only one of the eight brothers not brought before the prophet by your father? Why wasn't David in the house that day with the others? Weren't there other hired hands his father could have sent temporarily to tend the sheep?

As a counselor, I have heard innumerable accounts of the devastation that comes from a parent treating one child with more favor and honor than the others. Imagine your father saying to you, "Boy, go tend the sheep. The prophet is coming to the house." Then, as you are tending sheep, you see the pride your father demonstrates toward your siblings. He openly displays his confidence that any one of them could serve as the leader of a nation, but the only confidence he expresses in you is to be a herder of sheep.

Even if the prophet called you up from the group later, it would not erase your initial memory of the event, nor when no other brother was selected, your dad still missed the opportunity to present you to the prophet. Jesse never said to the prophet, "Oh my! There is one other son I don't want you to overlook. Let me send one of his brothers to take his place with the sheep and send him in. I've got another son you might really like!"

Instead, Samuel was the one who asked, "Are these all of them?"

"There is one more."

"Well, bring him up," the prophet instructed.

Could this experience have influenced David to give so little of himself to his own children? From this biblical account, he certainly did not know what the attention of a loving father looked like. And a man can give only what he possesses. If he has nothing in a certain area of his life, then nothing is all he can give out of that part of himself. So David's years of extraordinary victories on the battlefield were followed by years of sitting in silence in the palace. He did not know how to nurture or talk to his children when they were going through pain, because he had no memory of anyone ever doing that for him.

SCORNED BY A BROTHER

Some people who don't experience quality attention and affirmation from their fathers or mothers at least have the benefit of support from other valued people in their lives. David, however, did not. As if rejection by his father were not enough, other significant male authority figures in his life either ignored or rejected him. In fact, according to Scripture, he was rejected by almost *every* male authority figure in his life—Samuel would be the exception.

Eliab, David's oldest brother, rejected him. This fact is significant. Often the care and mentoring of an older brother can be the next best thing to the interaction and attention of a father, especially an oldest brother who exemplifies the dad's best qualities. In David's case, however, Eliab simply followed suit with the same rejection David's father had shown.

When David's father sent him to the battlefront with food for his brothers, David heard Goliath's taunts and asked what reward was promised the man who would defeat the giant. David's question angered Eliab, who scolded him by asking, "Why did you come down here? And with whom have you left those few sheep in the wilderness? I know your pride and the insolence of your heart, for you have come down to see the battle" (1 Samuel 17:28).

I don't know about you, but the way I consider it, when a nine-foot giant is threatening to kill everybody, you get sweeter to your family. The potential of imminent death would normally cause us to let little things go and family members cling to each other. When your little brother shows up at the battlefront and a humongous homicidal giant approaches, you would probably pull him to your side and say, "Come here, kid. Stand right here. I'll take care of you." Instead, David's oldest brother turned and said, "I know your heart. I know your real motives and the cocky confidence you have. Instead of doing what you are supposed to be doing, you are looking for an excuse to stick around and watch the battle." So there, on the battle line, David's oldest brother rejected him.

REJECTED BY A BOSS

Not only was David rejected by his father and his oldest brother, but he was also rejected by his "boss." You remember how the story goes. David stuns everybody on both sides of the battle line by killing Goliath. In 1 Samuel 18, the Israelites return from the battlefield and women from the cities come out dancing and singing, "Saul has slain his thousands, and David his ten thousands" (v. 7).

How did Saul respond? He became jealous, suspicious, and paranoid of David (vv. 8–9). David's father didn't believe in him. His oldest brother didn't believe in him. Then his new authority figure, King Saul, became so jealous at one point that he started throwing spears at David to try to kill him (vv. 10–12). Today that would be the equivalent of rejection by your boss. Write this down: when your boss starts throwing spears at you, it's not good!

This kind of rejection, like the others David experienced, is devastating to both men and women. Such treatment can affect how we will act as parents and operate in other areas of our lives. Rejection can be devastating, but it's not necessarily a fatal sentence. Do these experiences explain why David was such a bad father? No, they do not. Obviously, he didn't have a good hand dealt to him to play, but that's not the reason he failed as a parent. David was a poor father, not because he experienced pain, but because *he never dealt with his pain*. When you refuse to acknowledge the wounds of your heart and then deal with them, you will turn to substitute methods for hiding and coping with your pain.

THREE WRONG SUBSTITUTES FOR HEALING

David is not the only person who has ever had a wounded heart. All of us have to deal with pain. However, great people face it so they can be healed. Others try to hide it and cope with it on their own, but they never find true freedom from the pain. Sadly, when you don't seek healing, you are not the only one who suffers because of your pain. This truth is evident, not only in the life of David, but also in the lives of his children. Because David did not deal with his pain correctly, his children were injured just as he was. He and they fell into the trap of dealing with pain with three substitutes that can never bring about a cure.

1. MEDICATE YOURSELF TO NUMB IT

Many people choose to deal with the pain in their lives by trying to medicate it. In fact, this may be the most common response. You might have even tried this solution yourself. People who self-medicate their pain look for something else to cover it up. David and his son Amnon both self-medicated.

As I said previously, David had sexual problems. When he committed adultery with Bathsheba, he failed to face those problems. Eventually, he passed them on to his children. In David's son Amnon, those issues took the form of compulsive behavior. As a young man, Amnon pretended to be in love with his half-sister Tamar. Out of that sexual compulsion, Amnon became lovesick over Tamar and eventually raped her. Then he threw her out (see 2 Samuel 13).

This is a revealing story. There is a major difference between the ways healthy and unhealthy people handle things. For example, if you put a substance, such as alcohol, drugs, sex, or money, into the hands of a healthy person, then that person will seldom abuse any of those things. They don't need them because they are not hurting. If they do fall into the temptation to abuse something, then afterward they will repent and turn away from it because they see it addresses no real need in their lives.

In contrast, if someone who is hurting reaches for a substance, then that person will abuse it. People who are in pain may not abuse every substance, but they will often become compulsive people with addictions. Obsessive-compulsive behavior usually stems from pain. Why do some people become alcoholics? The answer is not because some people just like the taste of alcohol. They become alcoholics because they are hurting. They choose alcohol to medicate themselves , and it sedates them.

Getting honest with yourself and God is the first step you must take to deal with whatever problems you face. You must get honest about physical, emotional, or sexual abuse you may have experienced while growing up. You have to get honest about your feelings of rejection, loneliness, or failure—about the fact that you have low self-esteem. Don't keep going to the bars to medicate yourself with alcohol. Instead, begin by facing your pain. Why do some people become compulsive with food? The reason is the same—pain. Food becomes another form of medication if you consume it in the wrong way.

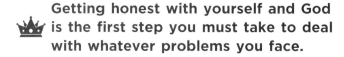

Getting honest with yourself and God is the first step you must take to deal with whatever problems you face.

It has been a long time since I have experienced any compulsion with food. Even so, I had short periods of challenge in my early ministry. Those early years were some of the most painful times of my life. I was filled with the fears of failure and rejection. I kept experiencing emotional pain, and I didn't deal with it by searching for healthy food. For example, I refused to eat anything green on my plate—unless it was green with artificial food coloring! I filled my diet with chips and dip, sugar, and cookies. For me, food provided the same comfort Valium or alcohol does for someone else. It helped to make the pain go away. I remember eating and telling Karen, "I'm hungry. This is what I want." The next morning, I would wake up thinking, *I really don't want to eat like that. Why did I eat like that last night? I'm not going to eat like that tonight.* But then I followed the same routine all over again. Why did I do this? Because I was hurting.

My behavior didn't change until the day I realized and admitted I was hurting. I was dealing with my emotional pain with the same kind of denial and self-medication that causes some people to become gambling or pornography addicts. They are hurting and don't know how to deal with their pain. All they know to do is to eat something, drink something, or overload their senses with something that will numb them and make them feel better in the moment. Even if it is only for a short time, for those few minutes, they don't have to hurt. Even if they have to wake up in the morning with that same "monkey" on their back, it seems worth it at the time. Self-medicating is a common response to emotional wounds—a response that will insulate you from the real need and postpone the cure.

2. MOTIVATE YOURSELF TO FORGET IT

Self-mcdication is not the only way people try to cope with pain. A second possible response is to motivate yourself by becoming absorbed in your work so much that you temporarily forget about your problems. Solomon, David's son, was a motivator. This fact is evident in the books of Proverbs, Ecclesiastes, and Song of Solomon. Observe all that Solomon accomplished—the buildings he built and the changes he made within the country of Israel. There is nothing wrong with seeking accomplishment—unless is done with incorrect motivations.

Solomon was an obsessive person. It is not hard to see what his pain was. His mother was Bathsheba, so what kind of whispering do you think had gone on around the palace about the infamous history of her relationship with David? Solomon was destined to become the next king of Israel, but his father did not set him up properly. Shortly before David died, Bathsheba had to remind David about his oath concerning Solomon: "You have another son trying to take the throne you promised to Solomon, and you had better do something about it right now" (see 1 Kings 1:15–21). So David made some last-minute preparations for Solomon to become king—preparations that did not sit well with one of Solomon's brothers, Adonijah. After David died, Solomon had to kill Adonijah in order to secure his place as king.

By this time, problems among David's children were no longer shocking news. David's whole family had experienced pain and hurt. Solomon was continually building, establishing new alliances, and expanding his kingdom and influence. Why did he do this? Because the moment he stopped, he would have to listen to the wounds of his past.

That is not to say that all the pain we have to deal with is caused by the wounds of our pasts. Some pain comes from how we deal with our relationship with God. Let me give you a formula that will help you understand what I am saying: God's ability to talk with you about your future is limited by how much you will allow Him to talk about your past. The greatest threat to your future is an unhealed past.

The greatest threat to your future is an unhealed past.

You may plead with the Lord, "O God, I know I have a great destiny. I want to go into the future." But you don't like hearing His reply: "I want to talk to you about your past, and I want you to open up and be honest with Me. I want to talk to you about the way you feel about your father and your mother, your brothers and your sisters, your friends and enemies, your teacher, and your pastor." So you get busy because you think God is asking you to face something very painful, and you don't want to deal with the emotions this would stir up in you.

For years, even while I served as a pastor, I ignored God in this way. I mean, I had a good relationship with the Lord. I heard His voice. I had regular quiet times in the morning, which I enjoyed. I prayed, read, and kept a journal. However, I generally tried to keep tight controls on the agenda for my time with the Lord. Then, 18 years ago, as God was preparing to give me the vision to launch our new ministry,

MarriageToday, He kept telling me, "Jimmy, I appreciate your quiet time. But I want *more* time with you. I want you to give Me days, not just hours. I want some days when you just sit with Me. I want to sit and talk with you." I ignored the Lord as long as I could, but He wore me down. Finally, I said, "Okay, I'll give You a day. I have some things to take care of, but as soon as I get those settled, I'll give You that time You want."

The time I promised to the Lord did not come easily. One day, I arrived in my office and thought to myself, *I have a couple of little things I'm going to do first. Then I'm going to give the Lord the time I promised.* So I walked around my office for a little while and tended to some things. Then I sat down for the time I was going to give the Lord and said, "Okay, Lord, I'm going to give You this time. I have no agenda. I'm simply going to sit in Your presence. I'm going to hear You."

No sooner did I sit in my chair than I noticed a filing drawer containing research I had started. I thought, *You know, I need to get that research drawer organized.* So I pushed myself out of my chair and walked over to that drawer. As soon as I put my hand on that file drawer handle, I thought to myself, *Jimmy, you are one sick puppy. Why can't you just sit and be quiet and let the Lord drive the agenda?*

Henry Cloud and John Townsend have authored a best-selling book with the title *Boundaries.* That book has helped a lot of people define how much freedom of access they will allow others to have into their physical, mental, and emotional lives. A boundary is a line that marks those things for which we are responsible. However, a boundary becomes harmful when it is used primarily as a defensive weapon to keep others totally out of our lives. Sadly, that is what many people are trying to do with God.

The difference between giving other people access to your life and giving God the time and fellowship to speak into your life is that God doesn't have any boundaries. You can expect to become uncomfortable at times with the issues He wants to address for the sake of your healing. He doesn't step back in the way others do when you let them know they are getting too close to the sensitive issues of your life. Instead, He moves right into the middle of your real issues.

The Lord says, "We're going to talk about Bob when you were seven years old."

At that point you might react and say, "Oh, I don't like Bob, and that's not a happy thought."

Then God says, "No, we're going to talk about Bob, and we're going to talk about Bob when you were seven years old."

Because of conversations like that, we often avoid getting alone with the Lord in any meaningful way: because He has no boundaries. God doesn't play by the rules—He makes the rules. That is why I found it so hard to give Him quality time with me. He desired it and knew I needed it. But I had some places where I didn't want to go, and I knew if I sat still with God, then He was going straight to those places.

I finally sat down and said to the Lord, "Well, Lord, I'm sick. I know You've been telling me to sit down with You and to be still and quiet, and I have been keeping myself as busy as possible. But I'm here now. Come into my life."

And come in He did, in a big way. He got right up in my spirit and started poking. It was in a loving way, but it still involved those tender places that He knew were so in need of honest attention and action. He started dealing with issues from my past, including some things that I didn't even know were there. "Okay, okay," I gave in. Then for several weeks, one thing after another, I began to repent and forgive and deal with these issues.

So what was the outcome of that experience with the Lord? In the end, He said, "Jimmy, "I want to show you a vision of your future." See, the Lord has a destiny for your life, and the greatest threat to the fulfillment of it is your unhealed past. You are the one who keeps insisting, "I want to talk to God about my future, but I don't want to talk about the past." It doesn't work that way, though. That refusal to talk to God about the past is one of the reasons people are driven and compulsive. They just can't seem to stop. They can't turn the radio off or the television. They can't sit down. Why is this so? Because when you sit quietly, it is not only the demons of your past who will cry out to you. The Holy Spirit will also speak to you and confront you about issues in your life that you can no longer mask so you have nothing left to do except deal with them.

3. MEDITATE TO DENY IT

A third possible response is to meditate—to dwell on your pain and rehearse your mistreatment over and over again in your memory. The Scripture teaches us to meditate on the Lord and His Word, but I'm not talking about that kind of meditation here. You might even call it *ruminate*, which means to brood on something, agonize over it, worry about it, chew on it, and puzzle over it. A cow is classified as a *ruminant* animal because it chews the cud, which means it keeps regurgitating the same food and chewing and swallowing it again until its digestive system can handle it. But God didn't make you a cow, nor does He intend for you to keep chewing on something in your mind that you can never digest. When you try an approach to pain like that, it doesn't go away. Rather, it keeps getting worse.

David's son Absalom did something like that. For two years, he sat and meditated on his brother Amnon's rape of their sister Tamar—to the point that Absalom justified murder in his own mind. He wasn't trying to pretend his pain didn't exist. Absalom was ruminating (or brooding) over it. Does this experience sound familiar?

The Bible says, "If you are angry, don't sin by nursing your grudge. Don't let the sun go down with you still angry—get over it quickly; for when you are angry you give a mighty foothold to the devil" (Ephesians 4:26–27 TLB). The word "devil" here is the Greek word *diabolos,* which means 'accuser' or 'slanderer.' If you choose to go to bed angry, then the devil is always at the ready to convince you that the people you are mad at are worse than you think. He wants to interpret and enhance their behavior for you. The devil wants to tell you every possible bad thing about them. This means that when you go to bed in anger, you wind up deceived.

A couple I grew up with—two of the sweetest people on earth—came to me for counseling, with each trying to convince me that the other was the devil. Do you wonder how someone can become convinced another person is the devil with every word and action premeditated and designed to undermine and hurt that person? They were going to bed in anger, giving the devil the opportunity to interpret each word and action over and over. Then each of them would wake up convinced because they had been meditating on those issues for a long time, giving the devil free reign to put his spin on it.

Absalom is a prime example of an unhealthy meditator. He would go to bed angry and rise the next day thinking, *My daddy had better do something about what Amnon did to Tamar. There needs to be a good hanging or execution. Then I'll forgive Amnon—at his funeral!* For two years Absalom stewed over these thoughts, with his father doing nothing, until one day Absalom decided, *Our father is not going to do anything about it. I'm taking matters into my own hands. I'm going to kill Amnon* (see 2 Samuel 13:22–29). And that is just what he did.

Meditators think constantly about every wrong thing anybody has ever done to them. You will recognize these people because they are full of hate and bitterness. You will see it in everything they say and do. In fact, they'll even advertise it. They're so full of self-pity because they consider themselves the ultimate victims. They will put their emotions on a mental treadmill until they are worn out with depression, bitterness, anger, hatred, and self-pity.

IT'S TIME TO DECIDE

Each of us has to decide what we will do with the emotional wounds and pain of our past. If we don't face them honestly, we will medicate it, motivate it, or meditate it. It will never go away until we do the right thing with it. It would be great if we had a manual to help us deal with pain when we are young. Of course, we have the Bible. Usually, however, at the time we experience rejection and pain, we don't always recognize what is happening, much less how the Bible speaks to those events in our lives. Many people experience incredible emotional devastation and don't know how to deal with it. That is the picture of David's past. Then we find him sitting silently in his palace as his family disintegrates around him.

Consider for a moment that a rape followed by a murder took place within his own family members, and David did nothing. Both of those events are devastating. But as far as we know, David never reached out to anyone for advice. He never sought counsel. David didn't bring his family together to discuss or resolve these horrific issues. Instead, he sat by silently as his family fell apart. David's inability to address these situations created even more devastation in his life, when ultimately one of his sons tried to kill him.

No one is immune to pain. All of us deal with it in one form or another. These are some most common kinds of pain people might experience:

- rejection by a father, mother, or siblings
- rejection by a man or woman
- abandonment
- divorce
- the death of parents or other close loved ones
- adultery
- abuse
- social rejection
- failure in academics or athletics
- failure in business, finances, love, or marriage
- physical problems or handicaps
- loneliness
- feeling that no one cares about you

For people who haven't yet dealt with their wounds, suffering in silence is what will hold them back from reaching their potential. Unlike David, many have not even experienced the first taste of their true potential because the pain is silently causing erosion inside of them. Others who have experienced a measure of greatness will not finish strong and live in the *fullness* of God's dream for their lives until they face and overcome the pain from their past. David and his family are examples, but they aren't good examples. They did not choose to deal with those hurts in the right way. For the right example, we must turn to another man who faced the pain of his past and received healing as he did it.

PAUL: AN EXAMPLE OF HOW TO DEAL WITH YOUR PAST

In contrast to David, the apostle Paul was a man who accomplished great things in his life, dealt with his past, *and* finished well. He was brought up in the Jewish religious and political sect known as the Pharisees, and they could be quite brutal. If you think of the image of someone "beating you over the head with the Bible," a Pharisee would fill that description. Perhaps you think you had it rough as a kid because you were raised in a legalistic, mean-spirited family. Even so, you probably couldn't compare your background to the apostle Paul's experience. The Pharisees were so hard and judgmental that, though Jesus never hated anybody in a personal way except the devil, He was very open about how much He hated the religious attitudes of the Pharisees. They could be brutal, murdering, and legalistic people. Growing up as Pharisee could be compared to being raised by parents who loved you when you made an "A" on your report card but never when you made a "B." If you experienced that kind of conditional acceptance as a child, then you have something in common with Paul's performance-based upbringing.

As a man, Paul (or Saul) was party to or even the instigator of the murder of Stephen, who was one of the original seven deacons in the early church. In addition, Paul was probably a couple of years younger than Jesus and could have been in Jerusalem during the time of Jesus' ministry, but he never darkened the door of a Christian meeting. Then, in the events leading up to Jesus' crucifixion, Paul's close associates were some of the ringleaders pushing the Roman authorities to execute Jesus.

Paul clearly had a bad past, yet in his letter to the church at Philippi, he celebrates his total healing from it. His example shows there is a way to deal with the pain of the past that will bring total healing. And that path to healing has three major steps.

1. FACE THE PAIN OF YOUR PAST

In order to address the pain of your past, first you must honestly acknowledge it—face up to it. Speaking of his own past, Paul said he was "circumcised the eighth day" (Philippians 3:5). Notice how, in dealing with his past, Paul went all the way back to when he was eight days old! He did this to demonstrate the background from which he came:

> Circumcised the eighth day, of the stock of Israel, *of* the tribe of Benjamin, a Hebrew of Hebrews; concerning the law, a Pharisee; concerning zeal, persecuting the church; concerning the righteousness which is in the law, blameless (Philippians 3:5–6).

Paul wanted his readers to know he was born into a family whose religious practices and political actions vehemently opposed and persecuted the early church. He even confessed that he was once an active leader in that persecution. Paul didn't hide from that fact. Instead, he just faced it. Paul said, "This happened. It is real. I was responsible. *This is my past."*

God's purpose in having you face the truth of your past is so He can take you to a good place in your future. The Bible says that He loves people who speak truth in their inward parts (Psalm 51:6). The Holy Spirit is also called the Spirit of truth. God is trying to get every man and woman, boy, and girl to a place of freedom. But we can only arrive at that place of liberty when we admit the truth.

> **God's purpose in having you face the truth
> of your past is so He can take you to a good
> place in your future.**

Sometimes we might be angry with the people we love. This fact can be one the most difficult barriers to overcome. We avoid looking into our past because the people we have the hardest feelings toward can also be the people we most love. We have a hard time admitting we have bitterness toward a parent who caused us pain. We don't want to face the reality that someone who held such an important role in our lives could also be someone who hurt us so badly.

Other times, we don't want to deal with people in our past whom we aren't related to—people we didn't love or care much about. We don't want to admit that a bunch of unlovely people could hurt us as deeply as they did. They are off having a great time with their lives while we are still broken. We are unable to move forward because we are too proud to admit their actions devastated us. You see, the devil will try every tactic he knows to keep you from dealing with these issues. Why does he do this? So he can hold us in bondage. We have to face up to our pain. But that's just the beginning.

The Pain That Comes from Shame

The human spirit is amazingly fragile, so much so that insignificant people often cause major damage to it. The feeling of shame can often be the reason we don't want to go back into the past. Even so, I want you to understand this: condemnation is always of the devil—*always!* There is no condemnation for those who are in Christ (Romans 8:1). A lot of people feel ashamed about their past because of things they have done: they may have had abortions, committed adultery, murdered someone, or any other act that would bring incredible shame. Others feel shame because of something that someone has done to them. For instance, even though they were not at fault, people who have been sexually molested and abused often feel ashamed.

God will **never** make us feel ashamed. Perhaps someone has said to you, "I'm ashamed of you." Nevertheless, you will never hear those words from God. If you have done something wrong, the Holy Spirit will convict you over that *specific* matter dealing with that *specific* action and He will require a *specific* repair. Perhaps He convicts someone about committing adultery, looking at pornography, saying hateful words, or stealing money. Whatever the situation, His conviction is specific, and His correction is likewise targeted and specific. That is part of the ministry of the Holy Spirit. He will come to you and say, "This is what you did. Take responsibility and repent. I will forgive you and help you overcome your pain." The Holy Spirit's voice is the sweetest one you will ever hear. He may be stern when you sin, but His sternness is like the firmness of a loving grandmother's correction.

What is the difference between guilt and shame? Guilt is a feeling that comes as the result of a specific sin as our spirits let us know we did something wrong. The Holy Spirit will convict (or convince) us of that sin, which should then lead us to repentance. Shame, however, does not focus on a specific sin. Rather, it is a lie from the enemy, which brings self-judgment and constant accusation. It tells us that we are defective. Shame tries to take something that was done *to* us or *by* us and then causes us to believe we have something inherently wrong *with* us. It is one of the devil's favorite tools. He loves to highlight unresolved issues from our past for which he tries to convince us that we should be ashamed—that we are just no good. Shame causes us to feel a sense of hopelessness because we may be able to change what we *do,* but we are helpless to change who we *are.*

Imagine how the enemy's voice would have sounded in Paul's ear:

> You ought to be ashamed for standing silently by and watching Stephen be stoned to death. How can you call yourself a "man of God," but then you condoned murder? So now you think you can you go around preaching in churches after you have killed people? There's something wrong with you, Paul. You're a sick man, and you can never qualify to serve God.

Shame wants you to agree with the devil's lie that you are unworthy and there is no hope for you. Why do you think the devil tries so hard to get you to believe this lie? He does it so you will not pursue an intimate relationship with your heavenly Father. It causes you to say, "There's something so wrong with me that I can't even go to God."

Because of shame, you won't come to God and say, "Daddy, look at this big wound the devil put on my head. Would you doctor it up?" Instead, you believe that you deserved what happened. You may think, *I know what that person did to me was wrong, but I should have done something. There is something wrong with me. I shouldn't have been there. I should have done something different. I deserved what happened. I'm so ashamed.* In all of this, God is crying out to you, "Come here, child. I love you. You have a destiny, and I want to take you into the future I have planned for you. I want to talk to you. I want to help you get free from that bondage."

But because of shame, we fear intimacy with God and block out His voice. There was a time in my life when I was wrestling with shame. Then the Lord came and I could actually hear the His loving voice speaking to my heart and wooing me to come to Him. I remember thinking to myself that I was deceived because there was no way God could love me in my condition. But He did! You cannot get free, healed, and ready for greatness until you get into the presence of this loving God. And when you need Him most, you deserve Him the least. That is why His grace is so wonderful.

God loves us just as we are, but He loves us too much to leave us that way. He is ready to receive you in any state you are in. God will not reject or shame you—ever! He is your loving Father, and His perfect love will cast shame, fear, and pain out of your life. But you must be honest and open your life to God. His response to your honesty will always be the same. He likes when people deal in truth because that is what gives Him the freedom to bring healing into their lives. As Psalm 51:6 says,

> Behold, You desire truth in the inward parts,
> And in the hidden *part* You will make me to know wisdom.

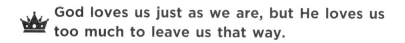

God loves us just as we are, but He loves us too much to leave us that way.

Everyone has done wrong things, including David and Paul. That also includes you and me. Every great person must deal with the pain of the past. That is because if you lack honesty about issues of your past, then God won't reveal the details of your future. A lack of honesty before God is the single greatest threat to the fulfillment of His destiny for your life.

The past controls more people than anything else in their lives does. In addition, if you are controlled by the past, then you are not being led by the Lord. So face the past—talk about it. That doesn't mean you should wallow in self-pity. Instead, it means getting alone in prayer and saying,

> Heavenly Father, I will go anywhere with You. You set the agenda. If You want to talk about the situation with Bob when I was seven years old, then we'll talk about Bob. I don't like him, but I know I need to forgive him, and You are going to have to help me. I'll go wherever You take me because You know what I must face to become totally free. I understand that You don't want my dreams and destiny to be compromised by my past—and neither do I.

2. FORGIVE AND FORGET

Once you have faced your past, what do you do now? After great men and women face the pain of their past, they *forgive it and forget it.* Paul wrote in Philippians 3:13–15:

> Brethren, I do not count myself to have apprehended; but one thing *I do*, forgetting those things which are behind and reaching forward to those things which are ahead. I press toward the goal for the prize of the upward call of God in Christ Jesus. Therefore let us, as many as are mature, have this mind; and if in anything you think otherwise, God will reveal even this to you.

"Forgetting those things which are behind" doesn't mean you simply erase your memory. Paul didn't do that. Otherwise, he could not have written about all the things that were behind him. Healthy people don't have the ability to erase their memory. The word translated "forget" in this passage means to decide not to let the past have power over us. We make the decision not to keep an account of those things that happened that could keep us in bondage, and we refuse to allow the devil to use the past against our future.

However, forgetting is not all God calls us to do. Notice how Paul describes the process as "forgetting those things which are behind *and reaching forward*" (emphasis added). The reason we are to forget is to free us to move forward toward God's destiny. Forward motion is a goal that begins with *forgetting* things that lie behind. That means resolving every issue. Confess to God every issue you have attached regret to and accept His forgiveness by faith. Don't let the devil condemn you for the rest of your life. The apostle John tells us, "If we confess our sins, He is faithful and just to forgive us *our* sins and to cleanse us from all unrighteousness" (1 John 1:9). When you confess a sin one time, God forgives you. The next time try you confess it, He won't even remember it. The Bible says He's removed it as far as the east is from the west (Psalm 103:12)!

The devil tries to get you to remember the past to keep you from approaching God about your future. Paul didn't tolerate that. He had been an active participant in murder. He had done a lot of terrible things. Can you imagine being in the same town where Jesus was ministering, and you wouldn't even walk across the street to see and hear Him? What if you were a young religious student, full of zeal, and you discovered that you had ignored the presence of the Messiah Himself while He was on this earth? Only after Jesus died did Paul ever start paying attention to Him. Even when Paul became a believer, he did not take the first step himself. He didn't get saved by attending a revival, walking down the aisle, and getting on his knees in repentance. The Lord had to strike him down while Paul was on his way to kill the followers of Jesus! Those are some awful memories and regrets Paul had to face. But what did he do about those memories? He forgave himself, and he forgave everybody else. He disarmed the devil's ability to hold his past over his life.

> **The devil tries to get you to remember the past to keep you from approaching God about your future.**

The most self-loving thing you can do is to forgive others and yourself, and the least self-loving thing you can do is to withhold forgiveness. Someone has said, "Unforgiveness is like drinking poison yourself and expecting the other person to die." Forgiveness doesn't make someone who did wrong suddenly right; it simply makes you free. If you are going to go into the future God has for you, then you must forgive others and yourself. You will have to get to the point where you are willing to pray,

> *Lord, I forgive myself, and I refuse the shame and condem-nation the devil has tried to use to keep me away from You. By your grace you are going to turn my mess into a message.*
>
> *I forgive everyone who has done me harm. I'm not going to talk negatively about them. I am not going to sit and meditate on the bad things that have been done to me. Instead, I am going to bless those who have hurt me. I'm going to pray for those people.*
>
> *Even if my feelings haven't changed, God, I'm going to trust You to help me. I will not seek revenge. Not only that, but when I have the opportunity to do good to those who have harmed me, I will do it.*

How does this prayer relate to someone who abused you? It does not mean you should ever put yourself in a position for further abuse. It simply means that you forgive them so you can go on with your life. Leave the judgment on them to God and trust Him.

You only have one clear path away from the pain of your past. Face it. Forgive it. Forget it. Do not let anything in your past have power over you. Make the choice now to forgive the past. Decide to forgive yourself and any other person involved in any negative experience. Then ask God to set the agenda and bring any other past hurts to your memory so you can deal with them. When He does, forgive those as well.

3. FOLLOW JESUS AWAY FROM THE HURT

The third step great people do with the pain of the past is *follow Jesus away from it*. The apostle Paul said, "I press toward the mark for the prize of the high calling of God in Christ Jesus" (Philippians 3:14 KJV). He also said, "I also count all things loss for the excellence of the knowledge of Christ Jesus my Lord, for whom I have suffered the loss of all things, and count them as rubbish, that I may gain Christ" (Philippians 3:8). All of us should settle the fact forever in our hearts that *all emotional and spiritual pain ends in Jesus*. Living in pain comes from not living with Him in a particular area of your life; it's a result of holding on to the hurt.

> **All emotional and spiritual pain ends in Jesus.**

Jesus is the Prince of Peace, and He gives us peace. He said,

> I thank You, Father, Lord of heaven and earth, that You have hidden these things from *the* wise and prudent and

76

have revealed them to babes [or people who are dependent upon God]. Even so, Father, for it seemed good in your sight. All things have been delivered to Me by My Father and no one knows the Son except the Father. Nor does anyone know the Father except the Son, and *the one* to whom the Son wills to reveal *Him*. Come to Me, all *you* who labor and are heavy laden, and I will give you rest. Take My yoke upon you and learn from Me, for I am gentle and lowly in heart, and you will find rest for your souls. For My yoke *is* easy and My burden is light (Matthew 11:25–30).

Rest for your soul means healing for your inner person. No more pain. No more medication. No more *self*-motivation. No more unhealthy meditation and bitter rumination. No more weariness and carrying the mental weight of past experiences. His yoke is easy. His burden is light.

Continuing to live in pain is the consequence of refusing to become dependent upon God in that area of your life. God's answer is for you to come to Him as a child. Have you noticed that children do not hide it when they hurt? They will let you know about it. In the same way, Jesus says in effect,

I reveal the Father. No one knows God except Me and the people to whom I will to reveal Him. He is a loving Father who reveals Himself to babies who are dependent upon Him. Come to Me if you're weary and heavy laden. I will give you rest in the innermost depths of your mind and emotions—I will give you soul rest. I am like a gentle surgeon. I am the One you can trust to show you the Holy of Holies of your life. The minute I touch you, your pain will stop, and the shame will end. For the first time in your life, you'll be free from your past so you can walk forward into your destiny, because My yoke is easy and My burden is light.

Every day you live with Jesus, you will get further away from the pain of your past and from the haunting memories of the bad things you have done. You don't have to live in the shadow of those things, because you are living in the greatness of the Lord Jesus Christ and in His presence.

THE END OF PAIN

All of us have pain. Don't try to convince those who have faced their pain that you don't have pain. You do. People who put on the greatest veneer to cover it often have the worst pain. What can you do about it? Well, you don't sit in your palace quietly watching your family become a spectacle in an episode of a reality television show. You don't become an alcoholic or a drug addict hoping that one day you can medicate the problem away. You don't work yourself to death for the rest of your life while your problems multiply around you. You don't allow yourself to be filled with hate until you become obsessed and deceived.

You go to God! You talk. And you let Him talk. Then you listen. You forgive, repent, and receive forgiveness. *Your pain ends in Jesus.* And when it ends in Jesus, you will be truly healed and ready for your destiny in Him to begin.

A Prayer for Wounded Children of God

Lord, all of us have pain. And none of us want to grovel in it. We don't want to live the rest of our lives dwelling on it, telling others about it, or medicating it. Some of the pain we know about. Some we don't know about because we've lived in denial for so long that we aren't even in touch with our pain.

Holy Spirit, we ask You to heal our hearts and minds. We ask You to help us to discover those things that we need You to mend and strengthen and other things that we need to forgive and bury so we can go into our future.

In You, Father, we have a destiny, a hope, and a future. We were created for greatness. Thank You for that destiny You have for our lives, God. We understand that You can release it to us only to the degree that we will deal with our past. So we surrender to You and ask You to come and set us free. We make the decision to forgive the people we need to forgive and to get in touch with the things we've tried to forget. We declare that You are the Lord of our past, present, and future.

As we sit with You in quiet moments, we want You to set us free and deliver us from all bondage. We stand before You unashamed. The things we have done in our past may have been wrong. The things people did to us may have been wrong. But we're not defective, because You made us and You're in us.

We declare You to be our King and our Lord. You are gentle and humble. And we trust You with the most tender and hidden parts of our inner selves. We grant You access to do what needs to be done in us. And we make the decision to speak truth in our inner selves and no longer allow deception to lead us into lives of ruin.

Set us free to our destiny, Father.

In Jesus' name, Amen.

Part Three

THE WORSHIPPER

PAY THE PRICE TO BE A WORSHIPPER

DAVID THE WORSHIPPER

MOST PEOPLE REMEMBER David as a giant killer, a warrior, and a king. They assume his greatest qualities came out in battle and in his role as a ruler. However, the signature characteristic of David's life was really in another area. He should be best known for his unashamed worship of God. As a priestly king, David exhibited the fourth lesson in greatness: **every great person is a worshipper of God and pays a price to be so.** As a worshipper, David's kingship stands apart from all others in four distinctive ways.

1. DAVID: PRACTITIONER OF PERSONAL PRAISE AND WORSHIP

David was demonstrative in his praise, singing, and dancing; he worshipped God with abandon. David's desire to worship set him apart from every other king of Israel. In fact, David is the only king God described as a man after His own heart. When Samuel announced to Saul that God had rejected him as king because of Saul's rebellion, the prophet said, "Your kingdom shall not continue. The Lord has sought for Himself a man after His own heart, and the Lord has commanded him *to be* commander over His people, because you have not kept what the Lord commanded you" (1 Samuel 13:14). The apostle Paul reaffirmed this declaration that David was a man after God's heart in Acts 13:22.

 David is the only king God described as a man after His own heart.

What would it would mean for someone to be after *your* heart? For one thing, that person would be seeking a relationship with you rather than pursuing you for what you could give them. They wouldn't be looking to gain a personal advantage from knowing you. Someone after your heart would pursue the part of you that you want to be pursued. How great does this make you feel? If you have ever been pursued by someone who simply wanted money, position, power, or something else you could give that person, then it's not the kind of relationship you really want. You want a relationship with someone who values you *for who you are*. And that is the kind of relationship David had with God. It is why God said of David, "He is a man after My heart."

If you are after someone's heart, you will probably try to emulate or imitate that person. You will begin to develop the same desires, characteristics, and interests. A child who tries to follow a parent's every word and action would be after that parent's heart. If someone followed a leader in the same way, then they would be after the leader's heart. So it is not a minor detail for God to call David a man after His heart. It had tremendous significance—God made that declaration for none of Israel's other kings. As David pursued God's heart, he became passionate and open in expressing his adoration of God.

2. DAVID: ESTABLISHER OF THE PERMANENT THRONE

David also possessed a second characteristic that distinguished his kingship from all of Israel's other kings: God established David's throne permanently as *the* throne of Israel. It is on this throne that Jesus sits even now.

Speaking of the coming Messiah, Isaiah prophesied that Jesus would sit on the throne of his ancestor David, whose kingdom would be forever:

> Unto us a Child is born,
> Unto us a Son is given;
> And the government will be upon His shoulder.
> And His name will be called
> Wonderful, Counselor, Mighty God,
> Everlasting Father, Prince of Peace.
> Of the increase of *His* government and peace
> *There will be* no end,
> Upon the throne of David and over His kingdom,
> To order it and establish it with judgment and justice
> From that time forward, even forever (Isaiah 9:6–7).

Remember, Jesus is in the family line of King David. God said only David's throne—not the throne of Saul, Solomon, or any other king of Israel—would be represented in His Son's authority and royalty. You see, David didn't only rule as a king. He was a priest-king. David was uninhibited in his worship. Remember also, Jesus too is a Priest-King—He ministers as a Priest, and He rules as a King.

3. DAVID: BRINGER OF WORSHIP TO ISRAEL

It is no surprise, then, that the third distinctive characteristic of David's kingship is that he introduced praise and worship to Israel. He brought in dancing and musical instruments and affectionate, demonstrative worship for God. Significantly, David introduced praise and worship to Israel not as a priest, but as a king. Before him, all the priests ever did in the tabernacle of Moses was slaughter animals and make sacrifices. King David brought worship to the nation of Israel.

4. DAVID: INSTITUTOR OF GOD'S ORDER OF WORSHIP

A fourth distinctive of King David's throne—and one that is vital to the Church today—is that God laid out the pattern of worship in David's tabernacle, which is the intended order or pattern of worship for all time. Acts 15:16–17 says:

> After this I will return
> And will rebuild the tabernacle of David, which has fallen down;
> I will rebuild its ruins,
> And I will set it up;
> So that the rest of mankind may seek the Lord,
> Even all the Gentiles who are called by My name,
> Says the Lord who does all these things.

Jesus declares that He will rebuild the tabernacle of David. No tabernacle before or after that one compares.

The tabernacle of Moses was a huge tent with several different chambers. It was large and difficult to move from one place to another. In this tabernacle, God remained hidden behind a curtain, which was then behind another curtain. Solomon's Temple created an even greater separation because the ark of the covenant was hidden behind thick walls and many different courts. The ark was the presence of God in the Old Testament era

In contrast, David's tabernacle was a small, one-room tent with the flaps up on the side. When he brought the ark of the covenant into Israel, he set it in this tiny tent so everyone could see it. All the Gentiles or non-Jews who came to Jerusalem could easily see the ark of the covenant, the very presence of God. In the tents and temples of Moses and Solomon, only one man at only one time per year ever saw the ark of the covenant. But in David's tabernacle, anyone who came to Jerusalem could see the ark at any time, 24 hours per day, seven days a week.

Why is this fact so important? Because today you and I are the tabernacle of David. It is not a religion or an immobile structure somewhere. Just as the ark of the covenant was freely accessible within the tabernacle of David, so too are we the dwelling place of God (see 1 Corinthians 3:16). Our bodies are tents that the ark of the covenant resides within, and our responsibility is to show everybody Jesus. God's work on earth today is not to restore a form of religion in Jerusalem but rather to restore men and women like David—people who are unashamed of God and willing to show Him to everyone.

THE VITAL ROLE OF REAL WORSHIP

Every person who would rise to greatness must clearly understand that God wants us to be worshippers like David. Worship is vital to us as believers, which we can see through five important truths.

1. REAL WORSHIP IS NOT THE SAME AS RELIGION

Worship proves the intimacy and legitimacy of our relationship with God. That is why true Christianity is *not a religion*.

87

Religion is works-oriented, which means it teaches us we should work our way to God through our own efforts. It then pushes us to attempt to be good enough or to try to figure out some way we can relate to God. However, this mindset is the opposite of real Christianity. Christianity is grounded in the reality that God loved the human race and so desired to have a relationship with us that He sent His one and only Son to the earth. Christianity is a real and personal relationship with God through Jesus Christ. It is not a religion of liturgy, buildings, and outward performance. It is a vital, one-on-one relationship with the Lord Jesus Christ.

♔ Worship proves the intimacy and legitimacy of our relationship with God.

Relationships forged in love involve affection and intimacy. And there is no greater intimacy we can have than with our Lord Jesus Christ. We would have serious questions about the intimacy of a marriage with no expression of affection. We would also have to wonder about a person who professes to believe in God but then does not worship Him. A lack of demonstrated affection typically indicates a lack of meaningful relationship.

Some people dodge responsibility when it comes to worship and say, "I worship God in my own way." Nevertheless, the Bible has already spoken about this matter. You can't simply worship God in your own way. God tells you how to worship Him: "You shall love the Lord your God with all your heart, with all your soul, and with all your mind" (Matthew 22:37). This means we are going to have to get over some inhibitions and wrong ideas about God and what it means to worship Him.

2. REAL WORSHIP IS FREELY EXPRESSED

Once you allow yourself to become more open in your expression of worship, you will first have to deal with how you will freely express intimacy with your heavenly Father, without embarrassment. As believers, we can express that intimacy on four distinct levels: *mental, physical, emotional, and spiritual.* Only in our worship can we express all of them at the same time. When I worship God as He wants to be worshipped, I will do it with my body, which means I will be physically demonstrative. My mind will be set on God. I will express emotions, such as joy, love, or thanksgiving. And my spirit will be open and in relationship with God's Spirit.

As I noted in the previous chapter, Jesus said, "You shall love the Lord your God with all your heart, with all your soul, with all your mind, and with all your strength" (Mark 12:30). This verse describes the way God desires for us to love Him. So if I take my body out of my worship and say, "I'm going to worship God, but I'm not going to use my body," then I do not worship in the way God wants. I also can't say, "Okay, I'll use my body, but in my mind I'm going to daydream about what I'm going to do next week." That also is not worship. Jesus, quoting His Father through the prophet Isaiah, said,

> "Well did Isaiah prophesy of you hypocrites, as it is written:
> 'This people honors Me with *their* lips,
> But their heart is far from Me.
> And in vain they worship Me,
> Teaching *as* doctrines the commandments of men'
> (Mark 7:6–7).

So I want us to settle something very basic about worship right now: Worship means I give my emotions. Worship means my spirit is communing with the Spirit of God. It proves the genuineness and intimacy of my relationship with God. On the other hand, a lack of worship is an indicator that there is something wrong with my relationship with God.

I'm in love with my wife. In fact, I'm so in love with her that it's easy for me to want to be affectionate and express emotion with her. If someone challenged me and said, "I just don't understand why you would want to talk to her in such a transparent, loving way," then I would reply, "You obviously don't know her. Because if you knew her, you would understand why I'm so in love with her and why I talk to her this way."

In much the same way, if I really know God and love Him, then it would be natural for me to express the passion I have for Him. If I did not want to worship God, then I could not fault anyone for questioning if I really knew Him. To have no desire to express worship for Him is a serious danger sign.

Loving God and worshipping Him the way He desires to be loved and worshipped means giving Him your all—physically, mentally, emotionally, and spiritually. To do anything less is a tremendous disservice to your relationship with God.

3. REAL WORSHIP INVOKES GOD'S PRESENCE AND POWER

However, worship is more than simply a natural expression of adoration and passion for God. It also plays a vital part in invoking—or earnestly requesting—the presence and power of God in our lives. Beginning a church service with a time for worship is much more significant than an ongoing tradition. When we worship the Lord, we invite His presence into the service and acknowledge that we are ready to receive it. "Enter into His gates with thanksgiving," Psalm 100:4 tells us.

A person who isn't thankful is never going to get close to the presence of God. That is not to say that person isn't saved or that they don't have God in their heart. But there's a difference between having God in your heart and giving God an opportunity to release the full measure of His presence and power in your life. Only as you seek Him can you reach you full potential for greatness in the anointing that has been provided to you through Jesus Christ.

Remember how Jesus said that where two or three are gathered in His name, He will be in the midst of them? (Matthew 18:20). He was telling us there is a greater anointing and presence in a corporate gathering than anything we can experience on our own. God doesn't intend for any of us to be alone. He has instructed us to be active members of His body, the church, and to attend corporate gatherings. He wants us to be dependent upon each other in a healthy way.

The instruction in Psalm 100:4 that begins "Enter into His gates with thanksgiving, and into His courts with praise" ends with this additional direction: "Be thankful to Him, and bless His name." Obviously, it is not to our advantage to be negative or silent. A negative person will never be able to enter into His presence. We are to be expressive, openly thanking Him and blessing His name— wholeheartedly!

By our expression of worship, we acknowledge God's rightful position in our world and in our lives. God declares that He is holy and is enthroned in the praises of His people (Psalm 22:3). Our success on any given day depends on the presence and power of God. We give Him an opportunity to manifest His presence and power by our free and open expressions of adoration and our acknowledgement of who He is and what He has done for us. To put it another way, without God, we don't stand a chance. Without His presence and power, there is no hope. But releasing His presence and power daily in your life isn't difficult. It is as simple as beginning to worship Him as soon as you wake up in the morning.

> **By our expression of worship, we acknowledge God's rightful position in our world and in our lives.**

Of course, worship is not restricted to the church sanctuary on Sundays. What we do in Sunday worship services is simply an extension of our personal worship to God that happens all week long. When you are taking a shower, driving your car, walking through your house, or working in your factory, shop, or office—whatever you're doing—there is always a time for you to worship the Lord. There's always time to tell Him you love Him and to be demonstrative in your affection toward Him.

Do you think that open expressions of your appreciation and adoration for God should work any differently than expressing how much you value someone you love? As I am writing this, I have just celebrated 39 years of marriage. If I have learned anything in all those years, it is that when I talk nicely to Karen, it is better around my house! I want to let you in on a secret: In the same way, when you talk nicely to God, your relationship with Him will be better, *and* it will be better around your house too. It is by your thanksgiving that you enter into His gates. It is by your praise that you enter into His courts.

If you grumble, complain, and do not give God the praise He deserves, then He still loves you, and you're still on your way to heaven. But there is a difference in the relationship, and not for the good. Your relationship with God will change for the good to the degree that you are willing to participate in praise and worship. This is the reason the devil hates it. He understands the power of words. Proverbs 18:21 says,

> Death and life *are* in the power of the tongue,
> And those who love it will eat its fruit.

That means you can release power from your mouth at any time, and you can reap the benefits of those words. With your words, you can build any relationship, and with your words, you can kill a relationship. You may understand how you can destroy a relationship by saying bad words. But did you know you can also kill a relationship by saying no words at all? Starving a relationship by saying no words is almost the same as damaging it by speaking negative words, whether it is with another person or with God.

Understand this: God has done His part. He has spoken to us. And His words are all good. When He speaks to us, even when He is correcting us, He does it because He loves us. His words are wise, life-giving words. But any relationship must be two-sided. Your relationship with the Lord will never be any better than your communication with Him about your love for Him. The greater the volume of good words, the greater your relationship will be.

You can't be the worshipper of God you need to be without being a verbal person. Even if you cannot speak with your mouth, your mind must speak to Him. We must understand that we can release power out through our words in good times and bad. You have been given the privilege and responsibility of invoking the presence and power of God into situations rather than just complaining about them or sitting in silence thinking about your problems.

4. REAL WORSHIP LEADS TO EXPRESSION OF LOVE FOR OTHERS

If you are a person who has difficulty expressing yourself verbally to the Lord, how do you break the chains of silence? One of my friends is a pastor in Michigan. He is a man's man. By that, I mean he's a sportsman and outdoorsman. He runs 10 miles every morning and loves to hunt. Even with all of that, the characteristic I most admire about him is how verbally affectionate he is toward his wife. When my wife and I share lunch with him and his wife as couples, it is not unusual to hear him say to his wife, "Love of my life, would you pass the ketchup?" And he talks to her that way all the time!

Now, I admit that I have been more inclined to say, "Karen, please pass the ketchup." It's not the least bit tender or romantic. I confess I have had a tendency to emphasize efficiency over relationship. But my friend takes everything he says to his wife as an opportunity to express his affection. I've had to learn a lot from him. Even more, he is also a worshipper of God and is open and unashamed, just as he is in his expressed adoration for his wife and children. It is no surprise that his wife is living in heaven on earth because of how he interacts with her.

I tell you this story to emphasize that **demonstrative praise and worship promote the healthy and regular expression of verbal and physical affection toward the other important people in our lives.** In fact, the way we worship God is often indicative of how we relate to the people we love. Generally, we become as demonstrative to the important people in our lives—whether it is our spouses, children, grandchildren, or close friends—in ways similar to how we are with God. If you are demonstrative verbally, physically, and emotionally in your relationship with God, then you'll find it is easier for you to take those habits into your relationships with others. But if you, through pride, fear, or other issues, do not outwardly express worship to God, then it will typically translate into a restricted demonstration of affection to others in your life, Because of that close connection between how we express our feelings for God and for those we love, take a closer look at the human side of this. I am going to speak specifically to men here, not because women don't also need to express affection, but because women do it more naturally and it's culturally expected and accepted. Men often need a little extra motivation in this area.

Demonstrative praise and worship promote the healthy and regular expression of verbal and physical affection toward the other important people in our lives.

Women Need Tender Affection and Communication

I'm not revealing a guarded secret when I tell you that women are different from men. While men and women have many similarities, their primary emotional needs are quite different. Women have several major emotional needs. For instance, women desire *nonsexual affection*. They want to be held and receive a great deal of tender affection, which makes them feel secure, valued, and connected to their husbands.

Women also have a deep desire for communication. They especially want *patient communication* with detailed facts about what is happening in their husbands' lives. Another need is for *verbal affection,* which includes frequent, genuine expressions of how beautiful they are, how special they are, how much they mean to their husbands, and how committed their husbands are to the relationship. Women will thrive on these kinds of verbal and physical affection.

Many men, including me, often resist expressing such feelings and thoughts openly. Our reluctance might come from past training, hurts, fears, or other reasons. I especially avoided communicating in this way when Karen and I first married. Many husbands simply must grow in expressing themselves for their wives' needs to be met. A husband can't start this by simply deciding to be a better husband. We have to choose to grow in our expressions of worship for our wives. We will typically not meet the needs of our wives for verbal and physical affection to any greater extent than we are willing to grow in our open expressions of worship for God, both verbally and physically. One leads to the other, and worship is the true foundation for all other relationships to grow upon.

Boys Need a Father's Affection

Not only do wives need those expressions of affection, but so do our children. They desperately want verbal and physical affection, especially from their fathers, but also their mothers. In John Eldredge's publication *You've Got What It Takes,* he writes how every child wants to hear from his or her father. Boys desperately need to hear from their fathers, "You've got what it takes. I believe in you. You've got the stuff." Every boy's worst nightmare is to hear his father say, "You're a loser, and you'll never succeed." The physical and verbal affection of a father is, from birth, extremely important to the mental, emotional, and sexual development of children.

My father's generation had role models very different than those of my generation. The primary role model for boys in that generation was the character trait portrayed by men like the famous actor John Wayne. His character trait was stoic—manliness was displayed by *not* showing emotions. Strength was measured by restraint, rather than expression. Sadly, this trait had a negative effect on many men and boys. Because of this past practice, many fathers today have difficulty showing affection or emotion to their children. Some men even fear that if they are too affectionate with their children, their sons will turn out to be effeminate or even homosexual. These fathers think, *I don't want to give my son too much affection because I don't want to make a sissy out of him.*

However, we have greatly misunderstood the real needs of our children and created exactly the opposite result from the one we really desired. Many fathers have unknowingly contributed to what I believe is a primary factor of male homosexuality. When a child is born, especially a boy, he needs his mother. But he needs even more from his father. A father's affection for and attention to his son, beginning at an early age, causes same-sex bonding, which is critical for a boy's development on every level. Without that bonding, combined with the close bonding to his mother, sisters, and other women in his life, a boy can become sexually confused— especially as he enters puberty. Because he has bonded closely with women, there is no mystique to them. Instead, he finds mystique in men, which then puts men in the role of the "opposite" sex. I believe it is the one of the primary reasons for same-sex attraction in boys and men.

In over 30 years of counseling men who battled with undesired same-sex attraction, I have never known one of them who had a close, healthy relationship with his father early in life. Though I am sure there are some exceptions, and there can be other reasons boys and men turn to homosexuality, the unmet need for attention and affection from fathers is, in my opinion, the primary issue. Every boy needs the affection and attention that will allow him to bond with his father and have normal bonding with women. Without it, even those who may not become homosexual often grow up becoming overly sexual, because sex to them is a way they can get the touch and affection they didn't get growing up. The affection and attention of the father has a tremendous impact on the emotional and sexual development of boys.

Girls Need a Father's Affection

Young girls also need verbal affirmation and affection from their fathers as they are growing up. They need to be held by their fathers. What that says to girls from a male perspective is "You're beautiful, wonderful, valuable, and worth fighting for." Positive expressions of affection toward a daughter show how special she is and meet two very important needs for her. First, it fulfills the important need for affection in her life. Second, it teaches her how to recognize a male who acts like a jerk later on in life. Every father is tasked with loving his daughter and showing he values her so much that she should never tolerate a jerk for a boyfriend or a husband later in life.

To put it another way, there shouldn't be some smooth-talkin' boy doing for your daughter what you should have done. She should not have an unmet father hunger that will lead her to constantly search for male affection and attention in unhealthy ways in her relationships. Lack of appropriate affection is the reason so many young women turn to promiscuity. They have a deep hunger for the affection and attention from a man who will make them feel beautiful, valued, and secure. So, if they have to pay the price of having sexual experiences before they are married, many of them will do it simply to meet their God-given need for attention and affection. Not only is it morally wrong, but it is also devastating their lives in the present and long-term. Daughters should never have to search for male affection and approval outside of their own homes.

Today, young girls' deep need for affection is complicated by the fact that there are many father-absent families. It may not be popular to say this, but several studies demonstrate that between 70 and 83 percent of incarcerated youth come from single-parent homes, and today about one-third of US children live in single-parent homes, usually without a father. Teenage girls from single parent homes also have a higher likelihood of unwed pregnancy, abortion, and sexually transmitted diseases. I am not scapegoating single mothers; I am simply stating facts that should lead all of us to action. Because many fathers are not in the home, for whatever reason, mothers need to find other reliable men who can be affectionate and give appropriate attention to both sons and daughters. Yes, caution is necessary, but don't let fear keep us from giving our sons and daughters healthy male role models.

I have focused on men, but I certainly don't mean to diminish the role of women in family relationships. As I said previously, women are more naturally inclined to have relational connections and to demonstrate verbally and physically their feelings and affections. In this particular area, women have a natural advantage, and I have a great amount of respect for them. Having said that, I would challenge every woman reading this book to examine her own heart in this area. Are you demonstrative in your worship of God? If so, do you then you show verbal and physical affection to your family—your parents, husband, and children? Is there a level of affection that you know you need to demonstrate, yet you find yourself fearful?

Even though women have a decided advantage in this area, it doesn't mean they have no room for growth. I have known women who showed very little affection to their husbands and even their children. In almost all cases, it can be traced back to unhealed father issues or past hurts in their lives. If you can relate to what I am writing here, then make sure you take it to God, as I discussed in previous chapters, and ask Him to heal you and set you free. Challenge yourself in this area and make sure you are demonstrating the necessary affection with God and everyone else in your life.

Our Marriages Need Our Worship

Physically and verbally demonstrative worship has an inescapable connection to expressing love to our families. Sadly, I admit I was selfish, prideful, and ignorant when I first met Karen. It is a miracle she ever married me. And when we got married, I was not an affectionate man, especially not verbally affectionate. Though Karen always asked me for verbal affirmation, I rarely, if ever, gave it to her. I had a lot of bondage in my life that led me away from being affectionate toward Karen, my children, God, and everybody else. A huge step in my spiritual growth was the result of moving from a church that was wonderful, but not free in showing affection or emotion in worship, to a church that purposefully gave God the worship He desires.

 Physically and verbally demonstrative worship has an inescapable connection to expressing love to our families.

The first time I attended Trinity Fellowship Church in Amarillo, Texas—the church I would later pastor—a man walked toward me to greet me. I stuck my hand out in front of me to shake his hand and to signal, *There's a boundary right out here, and you stay on the other side of the hand, buddy.* However, this man just knocked my hand out of the way and hugged me and said, "Good to have you here." My first thought was, *Hey, pal! You need to read that book on boundaries. You don't know me well enough to be grabbing me like that!*

After he (and others) hugged me, I sat on the back row of the church feeling violated. I thought, "This might be my worst nightmare." But everyone in the church was just as demonstrative. Then the worship started, and it was demonstrative too. Despite the fact that I was sitting there in total bondage and fear, I had to admit that in my spirit I was drawn to this new experience. In fact, I kind of liked it. I watched people all around me singing, clapping, and raising their hands, swaying and enjoying the praise and worship as I sat motionless in my fear and pride.

As we got in the car to leave, I was still thinking, *I'm glad that is over.* This was a terrifying experience. It's even a miracle we ever went back the second time. But we came back the next week, and the next, until eventually I became somewhat used to all these new, open expressions of love and appreciation.

One day I found myself thinking, *I want to raise my hands—* but I couldn't. It was as if I had 500-pound chains on my arms. I finally did raise them partway, but I was so filled with pride and so embarrassed to raise them in front of Karen that I waited for her to turn her head before I did. I was self-conscious about her hearing me sing or show affection to the Lord. Before long, though, the time came when I knew I needed her to hear me singing and for her to watch as I raised my hands. When I did, those heavy chains fell off my arms.

So many times, I remember sitting across the room from her, helplessly thinking, *I love her so much, but I'm an idiot—I can't tell her how I feel.* That's a hard way to live. When those chains came off, the pride and baggage in my life that kept me from expressing my love to my family also began falling away. My ability to express my love to God continued to grow, and it transferred to Karen and our kids. I am so thankful we raised our children with a lot of verbal and physical affection. I cannot express how grateful I am to be able to demonstrate the love I have for Karen, whom I love so deeply.

The experience of worship broke the iniquity that had been over me and my family. The value of that breakthrough in my life is immeasurable. But if you read between the lines, you also can see that it did not come without a price. You will see that fact in the life and character of King David.

5. REAL WORSHIP COSTS SOMETHING

In his later years, King David made one more huge mistake. He decided to take a census of the people of Israel. He wanted to measure how much military power he had available to him by counting the number of soldiers rather than recognizing God as the source of any success David had up to this point.

David's sinful lack of faith resulted in an awful plague that killed thousands of Israelites (see 1 Chronicles 21). After such great destruction, God stopped the plague, and as an act of repentance, David tried to set up a place of worship on a piece of property owned by a man named Ornan who used it as a threshing floor for grain. David made an offer to Ornan, but the owner offered to give it to the king at no charge. David refused to accept it, though. He knew that worship must have value; it must cost something. David responded, "No, but I will surely buy *it* for the full price." Then he added, "For I will not take what is yours for the Lord, nor offer burnt offerings with *that which* costs *me* nothing" (2 Chronicles 21:24).

King David understood if worship costs nothing, then is worth nothing. In fact, **worship without a price is false worship**. If it doesn't cost you anything, such as energy, time, or convenience, then it isn't worth anything to God. Would a husband or wife consider a gift without cost from a spouse to be special? They might be happy to receive it, but I don't recommend making that your anniversary gift because it's not special.

What price does a truly great person have to pay to be a real worshipper? First, consider the definition of the word *worship*. In English it is derived from the word "worthship." If you worship something, it means you find worth in it. If you worship God, then it means you will be willing to pay the right price to worship Him because He has great value—He is worth something. I don't know the right price for you, but it may be that you will risk losing a relationship. You may be rejected by your family or ridiculed as a "holy roller." You may even be ostracized from the people and the church where you grew up. None of those things really matter. Real worship tells God, "Whatever it costs me, You are *worth* it."

> **Real worship tells God, "Whatever it costs me, You are *worth* it."**

If you are unwilling to assume a wholehearted attitude to worship, then you are saying, "I've counted the cost and decided the worship God requires is not worth it to me. I have taken account of the resources it will take to express my love to God physically and demonstratively, and I just don't want to face the embarrassment. I have made my calculations, and pursuing God with all of my heart is more than I'm willing to pay." No, if you want to worship God in truth, then there is a cost, which includes four parts.

Turn Away from Laziness

Part of the price we must pay to be real worshippers is overcoming relational laziness and irresponsibility. In 2 Samuel 6, David recovered the ark of the Covenant and was bringing it back into Jerusalem. He intended to create his tabernacle—the one that God said would be the permanent pattern of worship:

> David gathered all *the* choice *men* of Israel, thirty thousand. And David arose and went with all the people who *were* with him from Baale Judah to bring up from there the ark of God, whose name is called by the Name, the Lord of Hosts, who dwells *between* the cherubim. So they set the ark of God on a new cart, and brought it out of the house of Abinadab, which *was* on the hill; and Uzzah and Ahio, the sons of Abinadab, drove the new cart. And they brought it out of the house of Abinadab, which was on the hill, accompanying the ark of God; and Ahio went before the ark. Then David and all the house of Israel played *music* before the Lord on all kinds of *instruments of* fir wood, on harps, on stringed instruments, on tambourines, on sistrums, and on cymbals.
>
> And when they came to Nachon's threshing floor, Uzzah put out *his hand* to the ark of God and took hold of it, for the oxen stumbled. Then the anger of the Lord was aroused against Uzzah, and God struck him there for *his* error; and he died there by the ark of God. And David became angry because of the Lord's outbreak against Uzzah; and he called the name of the place Perez Uzzah to this day.
>
> David was afraid of the Lord that day; and he said,

"How can the ark of the Lord come to me?" So David
would not move the ark of the Lord with him into the
City of David; but David took it aside into the house of
Obed-Edom the Gittite. The ark of the Lord remained
in the house of Obed-Edom the Gittite three months.
And the Lord blessed Obed-Edom and all his household
(2 Samuel 6:1–11).

You may have seen a representation of the ark of God in
the first movie about Indiana Jones, *Raiders of the Lost Ark*.
It may not be an exact portrayal, but the Bible describes it.
The ark was a gold box with two gold angels on top facing
each other. Where their wings came together was the mercy
seat upon which the presence of God rested. Inside the box
below the mercy seat a number of items were held, including
Aaron's rod, a pot of manna from the Israelites' time in the
wilderness, and the broken stone tablets from the first copy
of the Ten Commandments. Two poles ran along the length
of each side of the box to suspend the ark whenever it was
moved. Select priests alone could carry it and only after they
had gone through ritual cleansing and sanctifying ceremonies.
Each time they moved it, they would bow down and place
their shoulders beneath the poles to lift and move it.

When Samuel was young, the ark fell into the hands of
Israel's enemy the Philistines because of the sins of Eli's
sons. Nevertheless, the Philistines soon sent it back to Israel
after they discovered the power of Israel's God could not be
manipulated simply because they had possession of this holy
box. In fact, their presumptuousness only brought deadly
plagues upon them, and many died. It then rested in the
house of Abinadab for 20 years, but King Saul failed to treat it
properly.

In the years since the Israelites had regained the ark,
something happened to them. They became spiritually lazy.

Even King David attempted to skip the necessary rituals of cleansing and sanctification. Instead, he sent a group of men to bring it into Jerusalem. They were worshipping in their own way as they traveled with it but not in the way God had instructed. Instead of carrying the precious presence of God on the shoulders of sanctified priests, they elected to put it on an oxcart—in the same way that the Philistines did! How could they be surprised by what would happen next?

As the cart bearing the ark advanced toward Jerusalem, the oxen pulling the cart stumbled. It's no surprise that a problem would occur. In fact, everything humans devise to bring God into their lives apart from His way is doomed to failure. It's always going to cause problems. In this case, as the oxen stumbled, an Israelite named Uzzah reflexively reached out his hand to steady the ark. Immediately, he was struck dead on the spot. Before we jump to the conclusion that God is unfair, remember that the Israelites had clear and firm instructions. You wouldn't grab a high voltage electrical wire and think God was somehow responsible for the results. What might have seemed okay in human rationale was simply not following God's established pattern, so it produced a devastating, yet expected, result.

If you have laziness in your relationship with the Lord, then you will begin pursuing His presence on your own terms despite clear instructions otherwise. For instance, you may want to "fetch" His presence through your husband or wife. You might want your spouse to pray about decisions and then hear from God for you. Perhaps you will want to experience His presence through your preacher or someone else in your church. You might even think, "Well, preacher, we pay you to hear God." No, you don't pay him to hear God for you. You pay your pastor to preach the Word and encourage you to relate to God for yourself. You can listen to the preacher preach until the day you die, but it will do you no good until you pray, seek God, and read the Bible on your own. No preacher, parent, spouse, friend, church, televangelist, or any other program, place, or person can be your oxcart. God's presence will not be carried in your life unless it is carried in on the shoulders of a sanctified priest—*you*. And for that to happen, it will cost you something.

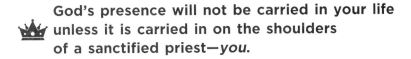

> **God's presence will not be carried in your life unless it is carried in on the shoulders of a sanctified priest—*you*.**

If you want to have a relationship with God, then you must take personal responsibility for it. You can't walk through life aimlessly and then expect to have an intimate relationship with the Lord. You will have to get rid of some things in your life that hold you back. You will have to repent of some stuff. And you will have to become more intentional about your life. It is the price of worship that is most precious to God.

How do you treat someone with whom you have a meaningful and caring relationship? I can't treat Karen in one way and then expect her to relate to me in a totally different way. If I'm going to have the right kind of relationship with Karen, then it will cost me something. If she is going to have the right kind of relationship with me, then it will cost her something.

To have the right kind of relationship with God, you must spend the emotional, mental, spiritual, and physical energy to *pursue* Him. You can't create an oxcart to fetch God. Every person who has a desire to be a real worshipper of God must overcome relational laziness and decide: *Whatever it costs me, I am going to pursue the heart of God. And at the end of the journey, I want to be called a person after God's heart.*

Letting Go of Misconceptions

The second price a person has to pay to become a worshipper is to overcome misconceptions about the nature of God.

After Uzzah touched the ark to steady it and died, David did not immediately understand what had happened:

> David became angry because of the Lord's outbreak against Uzzah; and he called the name of the place Perez Uzzah to this day. David was afraid of the Lord that day; and he said, "How can the ark of the Lord come to me?" So David would not move the ark of the Lord with him into the City of David; but David took it aside into the house of Obed-Edom the Gittite (2 Samuel 6:8–10).

David and the people of Israel had a misconception about God. Uzzah was struck dead because of David's sin of sending the men of Israel to fetch the ark of God without proper preparation. Uzzah lost his life as he reached out and touched the presence of God, as though God needed human help not to fall down. When the news reached King David, he could not yet comprehend the reasons for Uzzah's death. Not unlike many of us, the king sulked. David went back to Jerusalem, saying in effect, "I don't trust God anymore, and I don't want to worship Him. I'm not going to pay the price to get close to God. It's too expensive." This is often the response when sin defines our concept of God.

Out of desperation and confusion, the Israelites placed the ark in the house of a non-Israelite, a man named Obed-Edom. Then an interesting thing happened in that house. Obed-Edom was not killed, and no plagues visited his dwelling. On the contrary, during the three months the ark remained in this house, God poured out blessings on Obed-Edom and all of his household (see 2 Samuel 6:11)!

When this good report about Obed-Edom's household reached the king, a dramatic change began to take place in David's heart. Then he had the ark returned to Jerusalem.

> Now it was told King David, saying, "The Lord has blessed the house of Obed-Edom and all that *belongs* to him, because of the ark of God." So David went and brought up the ark of God from the house of Obed-Edom to the City of David with gladness. And so it was, when those bearing the ark of the Lord had gone six paces, that he sacrificed oxen and fatted sheep. Then David danced before the Lord with all *his* might; and David *was* wearing a linen ephod. So David and all the house of Israel brought up the ark of the Lord with shouting and with the sound of the trumpet (2 Samuel 6:12–15)

Obviously a major change had taken place since the disaster with the cart and Uzzah. Can you imagine how David first reacted to the good reports coming from Obed-Edom's house? Maybe he resented it. To David's ears, it may have sounded like someone telling him, "Boy, I tell you, Obed-Edom just won the lottery. You lost—but he won!" You might wonder what King David actually thought would happen to the household of Obed-Edom the Gittite when the ark was stashed there. Remember, this was the same ark that rained down a deadly plague on the Philistines and brought about the death of Uzzah. We do know that after three months of meditating on God's Word and having the opportunity to see there was nothing wrong with God, but with them, David was no longer surprised at the report of blessing instead of death for the household of Obed-Edom. This time, David knew exactly what to do.

He sent men to bring the ark to Jerusalem according to the commands of God's Word, bearing it on their shoulders by the poles as God had designed.

Six paces into their journey of returning the ark to God's people Israel, David saw it would be successful. After only six obedient steps, he stopped everything, made sacrifices to the Lord, and worshipped Him with all his heart and might. Sin no longer distorted David's concept of God, nor did it hold him back from worshipping God in the way the Lord wanted to receive it.

If sin defines your concept of God, you won't worship Him. But if Scripture defines your concept of God, you will worship Him with all your might. Don't let what your parents did or didn't do define who God is to you. Don't let the sins of people who have failed you define Him. Don't allow any church, spiritual leader, or religious system that has disappointed you define Him. Let the Word of God define who He is to you. When you understand Him according to His Word, you will worship this God. He's worth dancing over. He's worth anything you give to Him.

Lay Down Your Desire to Size Up God

The reason some of us are unexpressive or stoic in our worship and other areas of our relationship with God is because we are still sizing Him up. The third part of the price we must pay for real worship is laying down that desire. We are thinking, *Can I trust Him despite this terrible thing that happened to me? Can I trust Him despite the legalism, or the abuse, or the abandonment, or the pain in my past? Can I trust that God?* You might even tell others about God's love, but you aren't convinced that He loves *you.* Then sin is still defining who God is for you. Instead of believing God, you may be listening to all the wonderful things He is doing in the lives of other people, but you aren't sure that He wants to do anything for you.

Can you imagine how careful the household of Obed-Edom must have been with the ark after what had recently happened to the Philistines and to Uzzah? I can guarantee there wasn't any cussing in that house for those three months! They began to fear the Lord in Obed-Edom's house, and because of that, his household was blessed. At first David in his anger may have said, "I can't figure this out!" But finally, he read the Word of God and said, "This is how God wants us to treat His presence."

All worship is an act of faith in two important ways. First, it is belief in what the Word of God says about God, because this will lead us to real worship. Second, it is belief in what the Word of God says about us.

The reason many people don't worship is because, while they do believe God is a good God, they do not believe they are good enough to worship a good God. They do not believe He is willing to accept their worship after all the wrong things they have done. But remember, not everything David did was good. We can never do so many bad things that God will not value our worship—it is the most precious thing we can ever give Him. He values us more than we could possibly understand.

> **We can never do so many bad things that God will not value our worship—it is the most precious thing we can ever give Him.**

After making a foolish blunder that cost a man's life, David didn't give up. He went back to seeking the presence of God and in doing so discovered God's love. God blessed him because David's began to base his concept of God and his behavior on Scripture, not on misconceptions, laziness, or sin.

111

We must worship the God of the Bible. We can't worship a god of our past. We have to worship the true God for our worship to be real. We can't worship a false god created from beliefs not based on the Word. The Bible says Jesus washes His bride with the washing of water by the Word (Ephesians 5:26). The more Scripture you get into your heart and mind, the more nonsense you will get out. The Word of God will heal and deliver you. Psalm 107:20 says,

He sent His word and healed them,

And delivered *them* from their destructions.

God's Word comes into our lives and washes us. When that happens, it is as if a lens is being cleaned. Before the Word washes you, you see God as in a mirror dimly, but after being washed, you can see Him face to face (1 Corinthians 13:12). Why is this true? Because the Word of God washes away misconceptions, and the more clearly you see Him, the more you will love Him. Always remember, you enter God's presence by grace, not by your own merit. God only relates to you based on the blood of Jesus. Like David, you can worship God freely and fully in spite of your sins and failures.

Overcoming the Fear of People

The instruction on the price we must pay for real worship does not end here. There is one more thing we must overcome to be real worshippers of God, and that is the fear of other people.

Now as the ark of the Lord came into the City of David, Michal, Saul's daughter, looked through a window and saw King David leaping and whirling before the Lord; and she despised him in her heart. So they brought the ark of the Lord, and set it in its place in the midst of the tabernacle that David had erected for it. Then David offered burnt offerings and peace offerings before the Lord. And when David had finished offering burnt offerings and peace offerings, he blessed the people in the name of the Lord of hosts. Then he distributed among all the people, among the whole multitude of Israel, both the women and the men, to everyone a loaf of bread, a piece *of meat*, and a cake of raisins. So all the people departed, everyone to his house.

Then David returned to bless his household. And Michal the daughter of Saul came out to meet David, and said, "How glorious was the king of Israel today, uncovering himself today in the eyes of the maids of his servants, as one of the base fellows shamelessly uncovers himself!"

So David said to Michal, "*It was* before the Lord, who chose me instead of your father and all his house, to appoint me ruler over the people of the Lord, over Israel. Therefore I will play *music* before the Lord. And I will be even more undignified than this, and will be humble in my own sight. But as for the maidservants of whom you have spoken, by them I will be held in honor."

Therefore Michal the daughter of Saul had no children to the day of her death (2 Samuel 6:16–23).

If you will not worship God because you fear what others will think of you, you will lose a great blessing from Him. You will always have spiritual barrenness. Remember, Michal was the daughter of King Saul, who was a halfhearted, arrogant man who refused to obey God. So his daughter was not raised around a humble, demonstrative man such as David. What offended Michal about David's celebration before the ark was the fact that he had taken off his kingly garment and was wearing a linen ephod—the clothing of a worship leader. Seeing David parade around without his kingly garments affected her the way some people might feel if the pope ran through the city wearing a jogging suit. As Michal watched David coming into Jerusalem whirling around and dancing, she was thinking, *Oh my, he's not wearing his kingly uniform. He's down there in casual clothing whirling around like an idiot!*

After King David saw the ark finally put in place in the tabernacle, he came home to bless his family and encountered an irate wife. Michal scolded him: "Like a foolish person, you have shamed yourself before all Israel today!" David could not apologize or back down from what was born out of a pure heart before God. "I'm sorry you think that, but it is not true," he said. "And I will not stop worshipping God. In fact, it's going to get even more undignified than this." There is a fear of people that we have to overcome for real worship.

Often, if we fear what others think, we have the hardest time facing the disapproval of our loved ones. Even so, David refused to stop worshipping God because of his wife's reaction. He said, "You say I shamed myself with love, praise, and worship. But God loves it. And the people don't think like you do. They don't shame me because of my love for God."

Michal despised worship that was open and abandoned before God, and as a result, she was never able to have any children. People who will not worship are always spiritually sterile. They never bear fruit for God because it requires a price to be paid. That cost is that we care more about what God thinks than what people do. We live more to please God than to please others. So also it is with churches that have refused to worship God in the way He wants to be worshipped. They become spiritually barren and dead.

A CHOICE TO MAKE

After I personally began to shed traditions and self-conscious-ness and started praising God with all my heart, some close family members came to visit our church. At the time, they were not receptive to the direction our church was taking. They would not embrace the openness with which we demon-strated our love and praise for the Lord.

That Sunday, as the music started, I prayed, *Jesus, please let this be a day when no one speaks in tongues and none of the most demonstrative worshippers sit around us. I love them, but let them sit somewhere else. I mean, does it have to be every time we bring a visitor or family member, the most uninhibited and expressive worshippers sit right next to us?*

Our family members at the time were unfamiliar with our worship and terrified by the service. They were wide-eyed and stoically waiting to see what I was going to do. When the music started, I had a choice to make. I could either worship God the way I normally would do, or I could focus on what they thought and try not to disappoint or shock them.

I decided to worship God because my worship was about Him, not them. After the service, they didn't talk about it during lunch. They just politely commented, "Umm, nice service," which really meant, "Oh my goodness!" Years later, thank the Lord, I had the joy of seeing those same family members in a worship service with us, where they were demonstrating their own love and admiration for the Lord.

The way you help a person who needs it is not by doing what he or she expects; it is by doing the right thing. People who are in bondage in their worship do not need you to be in bondage just so they won't feel out of place. Neither should you rub their noses in it, nor should you act "holier than thou." They need you to be free and authentic in your worship so you can help them become free and discover real worship. They need you to be a tabernacle of David, revealing God in a respectful manner.

My rightful position of worship is free of the fear of people. Not because I am more righteous than anyone else or because God loves me more. It is a decision I have made because I am so proud of God that I refuse to hide my love for Him. I want to show people who He is in a real and gracious way and in an appropriate manner based on the setting.

To do this, I have had to deal with the fear of others. Some people have called me names in the past. Others have accused me of being part of a cult. I've even had some people refuse to have anything to do with me because of the way I worship God. However, no matter what anyone says or does, I have already decided to pay that price. It is worth it to have the presence and power of God in my life. The more I have learned to worship God, the more I have experienced intimacy with Him. And after experiencing Him, there's not a person on this earth whose opinion matters enough to keep me away from worshipping my Lord.

Jesus said to beware when all people speak well of you. Sometimes people will not agree with you, but you must still pay the price for doing things God's way if you want His blessing. If the opinion of others is of primary importance and it keeps you from loving God in the way you should, then you've allowed that opinion to become an idol.

Every great person is willing to pay the price to be a real worshipper of God. Part of that price comes in realizing worship cannot based on our own choices. Real worship has to be God's way. It requires personal dedication and the willingness to establish God's worth in our lives in a way that is pleasing to Him.

> **Every great person is willing to pay the price to be a real worshipper of God.**

Part Four

THE WINNER

BE POSITIVE REGARDLESS OF THE CIRCUMSTANCES

IN THE PREVIOUS chapters, I described four truths about every great person. First, we discovered that every great person is made great on the battlefield. David became great when he was where he was supposed to be—on the field of battle. He fell into sin when he traded the battlefield for the rooftop with Bathsheba. We do not become great when we go outside of where God wants us to be.

Second, I acknowledged that everyone makes mistakes. Only great people, however, take responsibility for and become greater through their mistakes. Psalm 51 records the way David took responsibility for his sin, repented before God, and accepted the Lord's forgiveness. David was a bad sinner but a great repenter.

The third truth I revealed was from a part of David's life that was *not* inspiring—his dysfunctional parenting skills, which resulted in the disintegration of his family. David was a wounded son who did not face the pain of his own past and therefore did not receive healing in that part of his life. He was not a bad father because his own dad had failed him; rather, David was a poor father because he refused to deal with his wounds from that relationship. Everyone has to face the pain of the past to become a great person.

Fourth, I showed how every great person is a real worshipper of God and must pay a price to be so. In David's case, he paid that price by repenting of relational laziness, changing his wrong concept of God, and becoming willing for his wife to despise him for his abandoned, unhindered worship before the ark of God. Like every person who has paid the price to worship God completely—heart, soul, mind, and strength—David had to be willing to esteem God more than the opinion of others.

DAVID THE WINNER

Now, I want to move on to a fifth truth about greatness by turning to what is probably the most well-known story about David and one of the most inspiring in the Bible—the account of a ruddy young boy going toe-to-toe with a nine-foot foreign soldier. This story has given hope and inspiration to anyone who has faced an enemy who appears too large to confront or conquer. It gives hope to people as they battle life-threatening sicknesses, persistent addictions, bankruptcies, or any other seemingly insurmountable problem.

When David faced Goliath, success, breakthrough, or a turnaround seemed too ridiculous to even contemplate. David was not in the army. Instead, he came to the battlefield straight from the field as a shepherd. To say he was rookie would be an understatement; he wasn't even a soldier. Anyone who reads this story needs to get this picture straight—no Israelite soldier could or would do what David did that day. If he was a soldier, then it was an army of *one*.

David didn't win a victory because he had a military advantage. Nowhere does the Bible say that he was an unusually strong physical specimen. It never records any physical advantage he had over any Israelite soldier.

But as we read the story, we soon discover one important difference David possessed: he thought differently than other men thought. Any soldier in Israel could have taken down Goliath had he thought the way David thought. You see, David *thought like a winner*.

DAVID'S MIGHTY MEN

When David became the leader of Israel, incredible things began happening in the nation. And when David stopped acting like a king, those incredible things stopped happening.

In 2 Samuel 23, we read about David's mighty men. There were 37 in all. To say they were mighty is no exaggeration. The Bible records their heroic feats like none the world had ever seen before or has seen ever since.

Consider David's number one mighty man: Adino the Eznite, who in one battle killed 800 men. Think about that. If a man were given a sword and ordered to stab to death 800 vanquished opponents who were not going to fight back, he would have a hard time doing it. His arm would start cramping before he was halfway through. More than likely, he would have to give up the task before he was done. Yet Adino *fought* and killed 800 men at one time. The worst words any enemy of Israel could have heard at that time must have been "Adino the Eznite doesn't like you." This was one terrifying warrior.

If such an awesome fighter was the chief of the mighty men, you have to wonder about the reputations of the other mighty men. Verse 18 tells of another mighty man, named Abishai. He killed 300 men with his spear in one fight! The writer also mentions Benaiah, who killed "two lion-like heroes of Moab" at one time (verse 20). This description means they were great warriors. Benaiah became bored one snowy day, so he dropped into a pit and killed a lion. He also killed an Egyptian warrior described as a "spectacular" man (verse 21). When the Bible calls a warrior "spectacular," it means he was one incredible person. But think about the way Benaiah chose to take out his opponent. This incredible Egyptian warrior had a spear, but Benaiah faced him with a staff (a long, wooden stick). He took the Egyptian's spear away from him and killed him with it. Benaiah was so fierce that he thought, *If I take in my spear, that's not a fair fight. I'm going to kill him with his own spear. That's the only way I can make this battle fair.*

These were David's mighty men. Meanwhile, David's own nephew Jonathan also killed a giant who had six fingers on both hands and six toes on both feet (1 Chronicles 20:6–7). In other words, he was a freaky giant. This is only a partial list of what David's amazing band of warriors accomplished!

The question is *not,* where did these men obtain such superhuman abilities? It is too easy to assume feats such as those we just read about could have only been accomplished by superheroes. The question also is *not,* how did David find and assemble such an awesome team? On the contrary, the real question is, where were all these men during those long days when Israel was cowering from Goliath's boastful threats? Where were they the day a shepherd boy with no recorded advantages in strength, stature, or battle expertise took down a huge seasoned soldier of excessively superior strength?

The answer is that when David became king of Israel, men began thinking like he thought, and giants started falling. Spectacular enemies crumbled. David's leadership inspired a revolutionary way of thinking, which gave birth to a generation of warriors who accomplished incredible military feats.

Any Israelite on the battlefield that day could have done what David did. In fact, any person reading this book could have done the same thing if we were thinking the same way. In fact, it takes no spectacular feat to hurl a rock at a giant if you have experience launching rocks at anything. You need a decent aim, but that isn't what made the difference. The way David thought made it possible.

So the fifth truth about greatness is this: every great person thinks in a positive, God-focused manner, regardless of the circumstances. Only when we recognize this truth about greatness can we begin to understand the vast difference between the shepherd boy and the Israelite soldiers on the day Goliath was defeated.

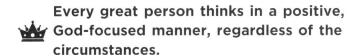 **Every great person thinks in a positive, God-focused manner, regardless of the circumstances.**

HOW DO WINNERS THINK?

The Bible says the soldiers who had been terrorized by Goliath's taunts for 40 days actually had their knees knocking in fear. Even so, any one of those men could have taken the same action David did. The real difference was in how they *thought*.

Consider again this amazing story, but this time, pay special attention to how a winner thinks. The thinking of winners has four characteristics or traits. The following is a long passage, but you will find it's well worth reading again with the concept of a winner in your mind.

And a champion went out from the camp of the Philistines, named Goliath, from Gath, whose height *was* six cubits and a span. *He had* a bronze helmet on his head, and he *was* armed with a coat of mail, and the weight of the coat *was* five thousand shekels of bronze. And *he had* bronze armor on his legs and a bronze javelin between his shoulders. Now the staff of his spear *was* like a weaver's beam, and his iron spearhead *weighed* six hundred shekels; and a shield-bearer went before him. Then he stood and cried out to the armies of Israel, and said to them, "Why have you come out to line up for battle? *Am* I not a Philistine, and you the servants of Saul? Choose a man for yourselves, and let him come down to me. If he is able to fight with me and kill me, then we will be your servants. But if I prevail against him and kill him, then you shall be our servants and serve us." And the Philistine said, "I defy the armies of Israel this day; give me a man, that we may fight together." When Saul and all Israel heard these words of the Philistine, they were dismayed and greatly afraid....

Israel and the Philistines had drawn up in battle array, army against army. And David left his supplies in the hand of the supply keeper, ran to the army, and came and greeted his brothers. Then as he talked with them, there was the champion, the Philistine of Gath, Goliath by name, coming up from the armies of the Philistines; and he spoke according to the same words. So David heard *them*. And all the men of Israel, when they saw the man, fled from him and were dreadfully afraid. So the men of Israel said, "Have you seen this man who has come up? Surely he has come up to defy Israel; and it shall be *that* the man who kills him the king will enrich with great riches, will give him his daughter, and give his father's house exemption *from taxes* in Israel."

Then David spoke to the men who stood by him, saying, "What shall be done for the man who kills this Philistine and takes away the reproach from Israel? For who *is* this uncircumcised Philistine, that he should defy the armies of the living God?"

And the people answered him in this manner, saying, "So shall it be done for the man who kills him."

Now Eliab his oldest brother heard when he spoke to the men; and Eliab's anger was aroused against David, and he said, "Why did you come down here? And with whom have you left those few sheep in the wilderness? I know your pride and the insolence of your heart, for you have come down to see the battle."

And David said, "What have I done now? *Is there* not a cause?" Then he turned from him toward another and said the same thing; and these people answered him as the first ones *did*.

Now when the words which David spoke were heard, they reported *them* to Saul; and he sent for him. Then David said to Saul, "Let no man's heart fail because of him; your servant will go and fight with this Philistine."

And Saul said to David, "You are not able to go against this Philistine to fight with him; for you *are* a youth, and he a man of war from his youth."

But David said to Saul, "Your servant used to keep his father's sheep, and when a lion or a bear came and took a lamb out of the flock, I went out after it and struck it, and delivered *the lamb* from its mouth; and when it arose against me, I caught *it* by its beard, and struck and killed it. Your servant has killed both lion and bear; and this uncircumcised Philistine will be like one of them, seeing he has defied the armies of the living God." Moreover David said, "The Lord, who delivered me from the paw of the lion and from the paw of the bear, He will deliver me from the hand of this Philistine."

And Saul said to David, "Go, and the Lord be with you!"

So Saul clothed David with his armor, and he put a bronze helmet on his head; he also clothed him with a coat of mail. David fastened his sword to his armor and tried to walk, for he had not tested *them*. And David said to Saul, "I cannot walk with these, for I have not tested *them*." So David took them off.

Then he took his staff in his hand; and he chose for himself five smooth stones from the brook, and put them in a shepherd's bag, in a pouch which he had, and his sling was in his hand. And he drew near to the Philistine. So the Philistine came, and began drawing near to David, and the man who bore the shield *went* before him. And when the Philistine looked about and saw David, he disdained him; for he was *only* a youth, ruddy and good-looking. So the Philistine said to David, "*Am* I a dog, that you come to me with sticks?" And the Philistine cursed David by his gods. And the Philistine said to David, "Come to me, and I will give your flesh to the birds of the air and the beasts of the field!"

Then David said to the Philistine, "You come to me with a sword, with a spear, and with a javelin. But I come to you in the name of the Lord of hosts, the God of the armies of Israel, whom you have defied. This day the Lord will deliver you into my hand, and I will strike you and take your head from you. And this day I will give the carcasses of the camp of the Philistines to the birds of the air and the wild beasts of the earth, that all the earth may know that there is a God in Israel. Then all this assembly shall know that the Lord does not save with sword and spear; for the battle *is* the Lord's, and He will give you into our hands."

So it was, when the Philistine arose and came and drew near to meet David, that David hurried and ran toward the army to meet the Philistine. Then David put his hand in his bag and took out a stone; and he slung *it* and struck the Philistine in his forehead, so that the stone sank into his forehead, and he fell on his face to the earth. So David prevailed over the Philistine with a sling and a stone, and struck the Philistine and killed him. But *there was* no sword in the hand of David. Therefore David ran and stood over the Philistine, took his sword and drew it out of its sheath and killed him, and cut off his head with it.

And when the Philistines saw that their champion was dead, they fled (1 Samuel 17:4–11, 21–51).

1. WINNERS HAVE FAITH-FOCUSED THINKING

In the Bible's account of David's battle with Goliath, the writer described how winners think. I can summarize what the Bible says by declaring that great people's lives are marked by faith-focused thinking. This is the first characteristic of the way winners think. This kind of thinking has two major elements: it is God-directed and reward-oriented. This spiritual principle is at work in Hebrews 11:6: "Without faith *it is* impossible to please *Him*, for he who comes to God must believe that He is, and *that* He is a rewarder of those who diligently seek Him."

 **Great people's lives are marked by faith-focused thinking.**

God-Directed

In the Bible, people who want to come to God must first believe that He is. He is here, now, with me. He is loving. He is everything the Bible says He is *right now*—not just in the past or someday in the future. He is the living God. Because He created us and loves us, we will want to please Him.

When David approached the battle line, his question included an important declaration: "For who *is* this uncircumcised Philistine, that he should defy the armies of **the living God**?" (1 Samuel 17:26, emphasis added). David's thoughts

129

were constantly directed toward the God he served, the One who identified Himself to His people by acts of love. When he went against Goliath, David kept saying, "You come against the armies of the living God, and this day God is going to deliver you into my hand." How could he say that? Because David's thoughts were directed toward God. He knew God was there, present and available.

Faith-focused thinking directs itself toward an unseen realm over what can be seen. The Bible says, "I have set the Lord always before me; because he is at my right hand, I shall not be moved" (Psalm 16:8 KJV). If we are moved, if we waver, it is because we did not set the Lord before us. The Lord promises, "I will never leave you nor forsake you" (Hebrews 13:5). That means the most powerful being in the universe will never leave our side, and He cannot be moved.

Who is this "uncircumcised Philistine" that comes threatening you, saying you are going to die early? That you are going to lose everything you have? That you can't accomplish the destiny God has for your life? If you are a faith thinker, you know, "God is with me!" You are focused on God, and you desire to please Him.

Reward-oriented

Faith-focused thinking centers solely and confidently on the fact that there is always a reward from God for doing the right thing. It turns away from the self-imposed paralysis of doubt and fear. It acts boldly, knowing God has promised to overcome any enemy for the person who does the right thing. This is the way David thought.

People who live defeated lives and never achieve any great thing always focus on the risk. They're always looking at what will happen if they fail: *What happens if I don't succeed at this? What are the consequences for me?*

That focus creates fear and paralysis. The armies of Israel who stood frozen before Goliath were filled with trained soldiers, including the men who would become David's mighty men. But they all had the same negative, risk-focused thought: *That giant will kill me if I go against him and lose. If I go down and lose—and the odds are great that I'm going to lose—I'm going to be killed. I would be a fool and a dead fool at that.*

David's question revealed a totally different focus in his thinking: "What is the reward for the man who does this thing?" His ears perked up as he heard about the three rewards offered by King Saul. First, whoever defeats Goliath would be made rich. That in itself was motivation for a positive thinker who knew God's promises of protection. But there was more. He would also be given the king's daughter to marry. And finally, his father's house (including his parents and siblings) would be free forever from paying taxes. The victor would not only be rich, but he also would never have to pay a penny in taxes on that wealth, and he would bless his family with the same benefit!

Every Israelite soldier was fully aware of what was being offered, but not one of them could focus on the reward. Instead, they homed in on the risk. David was so surprised at the magnitude of the reward and the paralysis of Israel's soldiers that he had someone else repeat it. "Wait, wait, wait," he said. "Tell me one more time about the reward."

Another soldier said, "Well, here's what's going to happen if you kill the giant."

Then David asked another soldier. Finally his brother Eliab heard him and said, "You know something? You left your few sheep in the wilderness just to come down here and hang around to see someone get killed and talk about how rich somebody's going to get."

"Well, there's a cause," David countered.

This is an important conversation. As soon as Eliab rebuked him, he turned to the next guy and said, "Tell me one more time what I get if I kill Goliath." And they said, "You get the daughter, loads of money, and a lifetime of freedom from taxes for you and all your family."

It was not long before some of the soldiers went to Saul with the report that a kid was asking about the reward for killing Goliath. For the first time in 40 days, Israel's leader heard someone asking about the reward instead of rehearsing the risks.

"Bring him to me," the king said. This was the beginning step of victory over the Philistine giant.

Now, I want to bring this story back to you. Maybe you are tempted to say, "Well, I don't want to stay in this marriage. It's just too hard. If I stay in this marriage, I am going to lose this, and this terrible thing is going to happen. I just don't feel like I can keep going anymore and keep trying to serve God. It's just too hard. It's just too much of a fight all the time. I just don't know that I can stand against all the temptation."

May I summarize what you are really saying? "The risk, the problems, and the circumstances are overwhelming to me."

You are ignoring the reality that there is a greater reward for doing what is right than there is for doing what is wrong. The reward far outweighs the risk in the eyes of God. When we begin to shrink back and give up, it is the result of focusing on the risk, the enemy, and ourselves rather than focusing on God's love, presence, and the reward the King has promised to us.

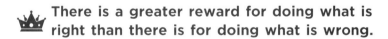 **There is a greater reward for doing what is right than there is for doing what is wrong.**

The Victory of Faith-Focused Thinking

The turning point in Israel's battle that day was a focus on God and an expectation of God's promised reward. One man, aware of God's presence and following after God's heart, asked, "What do I get?" One man did as Jesus would command: "Seek first the kingdom of God and His righteousness, and all these things shall be added to you" (Matthew 6:33). All things being added to us is a tremendous promise, and the one thing it costs us is to seek God first.

Psalm 1 says that if we meditate on God's Word day and night (in other words, if we keep our minds on the Bible), we will prosper in everything we do. The promises in the Word of God for doing the right thing are amazing—so awesome that the devil's only option is to try to throw us a problem huge enough to draw our eyes off God and His reward.

If you see God first as a punisher—thinking He isn't faithful, that He isn't for you and doesn't love you—then you will keep yourself continually defeated. That concept will keep you from doing the right thing.

No one is exempt from this tactic of the enemy. Every person faces difficulties. But as we do the right thing in spite of our circumstances, God will always reward us. He is a rewarder rather than a punisher.

You need to center your thinking on the fact that God is always good. He is always with you. He will never leave you nor forsake you, and He is a rewarder. He will always give you His promised reward for doing the right thing.

That's our God. He never moves.

That's the way David thought.

2. WINNERS HAVE FOUR-DIMENSIONAL THINKING

David also thought at a different level than everyone else around him did. It is somewhat humorous to consider how differently David thought compared to the Israelite soldiers who quaked before Goliath. They looked at their enemy and listed all of his advantages:

- Nine feet tall
- Bronze helmet
- 200-pound coat of mail
- Bronze leggings
- Bronze javelin, several inches thick
- 25-pound iron spearhead on his javelin
- A champion among the Philistine warriors (see 1 Samuel 17:4–7, TLB).

That's an impressive list—one much longer than David's. David evaluated Goliath, and the only thing he could find that was important to consider about his opponent was one fact:

- *Uncircumcised*

"Who *is* this uncircumcised Philistine, that he should defy the armies of the living God?" David asked (1 Samuel 17:26).
Not "Who is this giant?"
Not "Where did the Philistines find this monster who wears armor like a mobile fortress."
Not "Has anyone ever come within fighting distance of this strongman who wields a beam with a massive spearhead as a weapon?"
No, David considered only one physical attribute worth factoring into his battle strategy: the enemy was

uncircumcised! This is four-dimensional thinking, and it is the second characteristic of how winners think and how David thought.

Don't you think David picked an odd time to discuss a personal, medical issue? *What does being uncircumcised have to do with anything?*

Authority under Covenant

Circumcision was a sign of the covenant Israel had with Almighty God, Creator of the universe. It was a sign of a covenant of blessing. A covenant with the living God who had promised to bless the entire earth through Abraham. A covenant of protection.

Every other Israelite that day was thinking about Goliath's height, but David was focused on the one important fact that his enemy had no covenant with the living God. So what if Goliath was standing behind a shield that was taller and broader than David's whole body? The giant had no protection from God. David was saying, "That Philistine is uncircumcised, but I am circumcised. I know that I am under the blessing of God. I belong to God's covenant people. This is no contest."

Can I tell you something that can change your life? The blessings of God are in the invisible realm. There is a blessing for people who pray and do what God says. There is a special protection of God over those who walk under His authority. And that is the difference between those who are in covenant with God and those who are not.

It is not that God loves people who have chosen covenant with Him more than He loves those who haven't made that choice. God loves all people. However, when we become believers, we become His people. We fully experience the benefits of His love. We accept His invitation to live as His children. We are blessed with the privilege of walking in His authority in our lives.

 When we become believers, we become His people. We fully experience the benefits of His love.

Jesus said, "Behold, I give you the authority to trample on serpents and scorpions, and over all the power of the enemy, and nothing shall by any means hurt you. Nevertheless do not rejoice in this, that the spirits are subject to you, but rather rejoice because your names are written in heaven" (Luke 10:19–20).

Where does that authority Jesus promised reside? In the unseen realm. Where does God reside? In the unseen realm. Jesus said, "Where two or three are gathered together in My name, I am there in the midst of them" (Matthew 18:20). Though we may not be able to see Him with our physical eyes, He is no less present with us. To enter into God's presence and walk in His power, we must believe and live in the unseen realm—the dimension beyond our physical senses. This is the fourth dimension.

What Is the Fourth Dimension?

Israel's soldiers had taken their eyes off the covenant promises of God that existed in the fourth dimension. They had placed their focus and faith in what they could perceive and experience in the physical realm. On the battlefield, all they could see was a nine-foot giant flaunting his every physical advantage. They were hopelessly intimidated.

But why wasn't David intimidated too? It is because he saw and acted out of another realm—a dimension in which the promises of God were more real than the fears and threats of a human enemy. It was out of that fourth dimension David showed up and said, "You know he's uncircumcised. I can tell you right now he's uncircumcised. And in case you don't remember, that fact is not inconsequential"

I'm sure many of the Israelites were thinking, *Shut up, you idiot. You're going to make him even more angry by yelling that he's uncircumcised. He's probably already a little self-conscious about it!* But David didn't care what the other Israelites thought, because he had a covenant with God—and he knew Goliath didn't! Even more, David knew there was great power in that covenant relationship.

Years before that day, a similar situation had taken place. In the book of Numbers, Moses sent twelve men to spy out the Promised Land. Two of these Israelites, Joshua and Caleb, were men who thought the same way David did. Very likely, their story was etched deep in David's mind.

David had not forgotten about the 10 fearful spies who could see nothing but the huge stature of the people they would have to fight to gain the land of promise. They came back from their reconnaissance mission saying, "Yes, it flows with milk and honey," as God said. But all they could see was that the inhabitants were strong and the cities fortified. They saw giants there, descendants of Anak, and they were like grasshoppers compared to them (see Numbers 13:27–33).

Joshua and Caleb, by contrast, refused to be shaken by the risks. They returned and reminded the people of the rewards and protection God had promised for them. They gave a report out of the unseen realm:

> The land we passed through to spy out *is* an exceedingly good land. If the Lord delights in us, then He will bring us into this land and give it to us, "a land which flows with milk and honey." Only do not rebel against the Lord, nor fear the people of the land, for they *are* our bread; their

protection has departed from them, and the Lord *is* with us. Do not fear them (Numbers 14:7–9).

All 12 spies had seen the same things. Ten came back saying, "We have good news, and we have bad news. The good news is, it is a land that flows with milk and honey. The bad news is, we can't have that land because there are sons of Anak in there." The sons of Anak were giants much like Goliath.

Joshua and Caleb, however, shared the same facts but interpreted them from a totally different perspective. "We have bad news, and we have good news. The bad news is, there are giants in the land. The good news is, God has departed from them. They are not under the protection of God, and therefore, they are going to be our lunch!"

The people of Israel who had disregarded God's promises and limited themselves to three-dimensional thinking screamed, "Kill them! Kill Joshua and Caleb!"

The result? That three-dimensional generation was not allowed to go in and possess the Promised Land and experience the blessings of God. They all died within 40 years. But not Joshua and Caleb. The two men who had given the report based on heaven's realities were still alive and well, and for a very long time after that.

When they came back to that land as 85-year-old men, Caleb asked, "Joshua, where's my land?" And Joshua said, "I have some good news and some bad news. The good news is, you have inherited one of the best pieces of land in Israel. The bad news is, there are still giants on your land."

Without blinking an eye, Caleb said, "Well, let's go get 'em!"

So Caleb fearlessly went and drove out three giants, the sons of Anak. He was 45 years older than when he had first spied out the land. But that didn't matter. He was thinking in the fourth dimension, and Caleb knew his covenant with the living God had not changed. He knew he was still under God's protection and blessing, while his enemy was not (see Joshua 14:6–15).

The New Covenant

Joshua and Caleb unleashed the impossible just by believing in their covenant with the God who had brought Israel out of Egypt. But now we have an even better covenant—the New Covenant. We have seen the defeat of enemies much worse than Goliath or any other giant. On the cross, Jesus defeated Satan, sin, death, and hell!

No matter how the devil is trying to deceive you right now, he is doing it without a hint of protection. He might seem like a giant, but he can never be under God's covenant. You, however, are under the protection of the living God. So who cares what giant comes against you? As a born-again believer, you have been given all authority through Jesus Christ. You can defeat any enemy!

> **As a born-again believer, you have been given all authority through Jesus Christ. You can defeat any enemy!**

Satan will do everything he can to get you to think and act in three-dimensional terms. If he succeeds, you will be overwhelmed. You will be defeated if you let yourself focus only on the numbers in your checkbook, the problems in your marriage, the concerns over your children, the current lack of success in your business, or the sickness that is manifesting in your body.

But if you will think in the fourth dimension and focus on the fact that the living God is with you and you are His covenant child, you can see the breakthroughs and victories God has for you on the other side of those situations.

The Bible says we have not because we ask not (James 4:2). Pointing to the day when He would go to the Father and finish His work on this earth, Jesus said we could ask for anything in His name and He would do it (John 14:14). So why don't we ask? Because we allow ourselves to be overwhelmed by what we see, and we forget that God is with us.

Success belongs to the person who, in the midst of the greatest opposition, will push forward in the knowledge that the enemy is without protection, is totally uncovered, and has already been defeated at the cross. Success belongs to the person who lives in that unseen fourth-dimensional realm. Great people succeed and are winners when they walk in covenant with the living God.

3. FRESH IDEAS ARE POWERFUL IDEAS

A third characteristic of the way winners think is that they have fresh ideas. Great people think differently from everybody else.

Remember, military warfare in David's day was done by hand-to-hand combat. My choice against a giant would have been an "equalizer" like a handgun or maybe a bazooka or rocket mortar. Even better, I would prefer to order a lethal drone strike from the comfort of my own home. Imagine going hand-to-hand against an enemy with a spear that is as thick and long as a fence post. That's big! It means that if you run at him with the size spear you can effectively wield, he will nail you before you ever get close to him. A sword would be no better. So how are you going to fight such an impossible opponent?

Perhaps King Saul had been thinking along these lines when he offered David his personal armor. David tried it on.

I'm sure it was shiny, good-looking armor. Saul presumably possessed the best armor in all of Israel. But the challenge was not to impress Goliath—it was to kill him. And even the best-looking, best-made armor did not offer a fresh solution to the challenge they faced. Goliath's spear would flatten than armor like an aluminum soft drink can. In fact, in the past 40 days, no one had come up with a new idea of how to kill this giant. Every man imagined his own chest caving under the force of that spear.

Then David showed up. And he had a better idea. No one else had thought about killing the giant without ever getting within his reach. David, however, decided that by using a projectile he could get close enough to hit Goliath without being within range of Goliath's spear. A second part of David's strategy was to be unintimidating. When he approached the giant, he carried not a sword but a shepherd's staff and wore a shepherd's garment rather than Saul's armor.

Goliath was insulted: "You think I'm a dog that you come at me with a stick?" The giant focused on the insult rather than the actual combat. He cursed David by the Philistines' gods. The giant's indignation and anger grew as David declared God's covenant promise to deliver him and Israel:

> The Philistine said to David, "Come to me, and I will give your flesh to the birds of the air and the beasts of the field!"
>
> Then David said to the Philistine, "You come to me with a sword, with a spear, and with a javelin. But I come to you in the name of the Lord of hosts, the God of the armies of Israel, whom you have defied. This day the Lord will deliver you into my hand, and I will strike you and take your head from you. And this day I will give the carcasses of the camp of the Philistines to the birds of the air and the wild beasts of the earth, that all the earth may know that

there is a God in Israel. Then all this assembly shall know that the Lord does not save with sword and spear; for the battle *is* the Lord's, and He will give you into our hands" (1 Samuel 17:44–47).

Before Goliath realized what was happening, the still air was pierced by a *swoosh* sound, followed by a dull thud. We could say that after initially being an insult to Goliath, in the end David left a lasting impression on his foe! The stone from David's slingshot embedded itself in the giant's forehead, and Goliath fell face forward to the ground. David immediately took Goliath's own sword and severed his head, causing the Philistine troops to flee in fear. Circumcision might seem inconsequential, but for Goliath it was actually a matter of life and death.

For 40 days no one had been able to think of anything but conventional approaches to defeat this enemy. They weren't creative thinkers. They were stuck in tradition, but it was a dead tradition. David dug back into the true and oldest tradition, and he declared that God's ancient covenant would manifest itself that day in victory over the enemies of God and His people. And a new weapon would reveal God's eternal promise to His people.

If All You Have Is a Hammer …

A motivational theorist expressed being stuck in conventional solutions in his maxim: "If the only tool you have is a hammer, you will see every problem as a nail." Many people go through life with the same answer to every problem. It's the same answer their mom and dad had. It's the same problem that everybody else has. They assess and address every situation in life with the same hammer. Even when it doesn't work 99 percent of the time, their solution to everything is the hammer. They don't realize that if they are not dealing with a nail, it is time to change tools.

All the army of Israel stood and shook in fear for 40 days over the prospect of trying to defeat Goliath with the same style of combat they had used before. No one came up with an alternative solution like David's: "The best way to attack this guy is with a projectile. That won't threaten him. All we have to do is go down and launch this at him."

But if we look at what Scripture says about David's solution, we can see that his approach may have been even fresher than it appears at first glance. It is easy to assume David was applying a technique he had used on animals that threatened his sheep. But Scripture does not say this. In fact, as far as we know, David had never fought with a slingshot before. Remember, when David showed up at the battle line, Saul said, "You can't do this, son. You're going up against a trained soldier. You're just a boy. Goliath has been a soldier since he was young." David's response was "I took care of my father's sheep. And when the lion or the bear came against my father's sheep, I attacked it. I grabbed it by the beard and killed it" (see 1 Samuel 17:34–35). He didn't say that he ever used a slingshot. A slingshot was a new solution for a new problem.

Can I tell you something that you can hold onto for the rest of your life? Jesus says the Holy Spirit will lead you into all truth. That means He has the solution for your problem. That solution will always be according to the truth, and it will always be creative. It won't be a hammer for a screw or a screwdriver where you need a saw. It won't be the same old thing every time you face a new problem. It will be the right solution for each need. By His power, the Holy Spirit will instill a new creativity to your life. He will fill you with wit and wisdom you never knew you had.

So when you pray, you can ask specifically, "Holy Spirit, how do I deal with this child? I know what worked for my other child. But what about this child with a different personality?" You can pray, "I know what happened 10 years ago, but what do I do today in a culture that has changed? Truth hasn't changed, but the culture has changed. How do I reach people now? How do I share the gospel now? How do I succeed in business in a new and different economy? Holy Spirit, how do I do it now?"

Failure comes when people are more married to tradition than they are to the truth. They are using the same old armor even though the battle has changed; the same old tool even though the problem is completely different. But what didn't change? God's covenant to be present with you at all times.

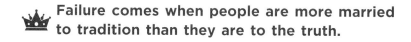 **Failure comes when people are more married to tradition than they are to the truth.**

Humility: The Starting Point for Fresh Ideas

One reason David was free to take a fresh approach was because he was humble. The Bible says,

> God resists the proud
> But gives grace to the humble (James 4:6).

There was probably not any soldier in Israel that day who would have been willing to attack the giant without wearing armor, because they all knew they would have been ridiculed.

I'm sure David looked good wearing the king's armor and carrying the king's sword. But he was willing to acknowledge that looking good was not going to put him in a better position to achieve the real goal.

Many people would rather look good losing than suffer the ridicule that may come with doing something differently in order to succeed. David took off Saul's armor, saying, "I'm sorry, I've never used this stuff before, and I'm not comfortable with it." He was willing to be an outcast among the soldiers of Israel and be despised by an insulted Goliath. But the moment came when he was the one standing with Goliath's head dangling from his hand! In that instant David became a genius to all who doubted. He had trained himself to think like great people think. He thought about the rewards God promised to those in covenant with Him. And an essential element of that kind of thinking is having fresh ideas.

How do you get fresh thinking? You humble yourself and ask God. Then you must be willing to become an innovator when the Holy Spirit speaks to you and leads you. He will never tell you anything that is inconsistent with Scripture, but He will tell you something that's right for the moment— right for now. A fresh approach always works when God originates it. It is always the right answer for what you need. Every great person is open to fresh ideas.

Yes, people may talk about you or ridicule you. Yes, you may face some initial opposition. And that is the reason there is a fourth essential characteristic of the thinking of every winner.

4. FORCEFUL THINKING

I have already written that David had three key elements to his thinking that are characteristic of the thinking of every winner. Through faith, he focused on God and did not allow the risks to draw his eye away from the rewards. He thought four dimensionally, allowing the unseen realm of what God has promised to turn around any situation. And his humility allowed him to come up with new approaches when conventional ones didn't work.

But as creative and clear thinking as David was, his great ideas would have come to nothing if he had not also been a forceful thinker, which is the fourth characteristic of the way a winner thinks. The fact is, if you are a weak thinker—willing to give up the first time someone tells you that your approach is not going to work—you will never make it in life. Winners think in forceful terms. They have to.

The Inevitability of Resistance

Let's do a quick review of the opposition David received in response to his inquiries and ideas. Three people came against him. The first was his brother, who said, "You've got wrong motives, you little punk. You came down here for the wrong reason." Then there was King Saul, who told him, "Son, you can't do this." And the third was Goliath, who scoffed at him. "Come down here, boy. I'm going to show you what I do to boys who run at me with sticks," he taunted. "I'm going to kill you!"

To achieve the greatness God had for him, David could not listen to what his family said. He could not accept what King Saul said. And he certainly could not be affected by what his enemy said. In each case, he responded in the right way. He was not rebellious, reactive, or presumptuous. David was simply a forceful thinker who refused to be swayed. Instead, he thought, *I'm not giving up on this because I know it is from God.*

Remember, you will never grow beyond or rise above the need to be submitted to authority. Stay teachable. But if you think that you're ever going to do anything great in life without opposition, you are naive. Never have I done anything worthwhile without some people telling me it could not be done. Nor has anyone else.

An example of this point is Lakewood Church in Houston, Texas. Their present facility was formerly the Compaq Center, which was owned by the city of Houston.

When Pastor Joel Osteen announced the vision of moving out of their old facility and acquiring the Compaq Center, many people said, "Joel, the city of Houston will never give you that building. It's a city building, and it's too big and expensive."

Joel responded, "No, I believe we're going to have favor from God, and we're going to get that building." He was right. They bought the building and became the largest church in America. God had truly spoken to Joel Osteen. But it wouldn't have worked out if he had not been a forceful thinker.

If you are going to achieve great things for God, you must accept the fact that you will have resistance. People may say, "It cannot be done. It has never been done before! Who do you think you are that you could do something so great?"

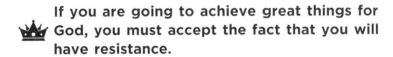

> **If you are going to achieve great things for God, you must accept the fact that you will have resistance.**

When you hear those things, respond as David did. And David never gave a wrong response. He never became hateful, acted unlovingly, or behaved in an unrighteous way. To a brother who accused him of wrong motives and selfish ambition, he turned and said, "Eliab, this is important." David may have wanted to tear into him, but he didn't act unrighteously or disrespect Eliab's position in the family. He just turned and said, "There is a cause here, Eliab. Come on. You know this is important." To his king who told him that he didn't have the experience and skills to defeat a seasoned warrior, David made a righteous appeal. First, he submitted himself as "your servant." Then he said, "God is going to be with me, and I'm going to do to that giant what I did to the lion and the bear." Based on David's righteous appeal, the king let him face Goliath. To his enemy, who cursed him, David refused to curse back or boast about himself. Instead, he pronounced the Word of God and boasted about his Lord: "You come against me with a sword and a spear. I come against you in the name of the living God."

David was a forceful thinker.

IT CAN BE DONE

Jesus said, "From the days of John the Baptist until now the kingdom of heaven suffers violence, and the violent take it by force" (Matthew 11:12).

You have to be a forceful thinker. That doesn't mean you should not be submitted to authority and teachable or that you should refuse to listen to wise counsel. What it does mean is that any time you are trying to do something great, you can expect someone to tell you it can't be done. The devil is going to tell you it can't be done.

When his father died, Joel Osteen said, "I knew that the Lord was calling me to be the pastor, but I had never preached, not one time." Joel worked in the video department of his father's church and might have been considered a shy, timid, behind-the-scenes person. He said, "So many times I would wake up in the middle of the night and the devil would say, 'What in the world do you think you've done? Who do you think you are? Nobody's going to show up to hear you.'"

It would have been a great accomplishment for anyone to take that church and simply maintain the success that had already been attained, much less double or triple it. But when the devil tried to cause Joel to be fearful and undermine his confidence in the middle of the night, Joel answered back, "I can do all things through Christ who gives me strength. I'm going to do this because the favor of God is on me, and God is going to anoint me."

Great men and women are forceful thinkers. David brought greatness in thinking to the nation of Israel. He was a winner who made his people winners. The moment he became king, everything changed. When every other Israelite had given up and refused to fight, a great person showed up and said, "We're going to get the reward because these are uncircumcised people. I've got a new idea about how we're going to win this battle! I don't care what the enemy says—we can do it." Then, after David had killed Goliath, the Bible tells about Adino the Eznite rising up and killing 800 soldiers in one battle. A generation of warriors and winners came up under David—a band of mighty men whose greatness was marked not so much by how they fought as by how they thought.

Don't think God has destined any person to do less. Don't allow anyone to tell you that you can't. You are someone special. A great God created you in your mother's womb to be a winner. You can accomplish all God has planned for you to do. Only the territory between your ears can keep you from it.

 You can accomplish all God has planned for you to do. Only the territory between your ears can keep you from it.

Part Five

THE WAITING KING

SUBMIT TO GOD'S AUTHORITY AND TO THOSE HE DELEGATES

THE SCRIPTURES EXALT David as a truly great man. Yes, the Bible does not portray him as perfect; some areas of his life were far less than admirable. Yet, in many ways, he is an example of what every great person of God should be. The key value of David's example was not his human perfection (or imperfection), but that he is recognized in Scripture as a man after God's heart. Perhaps the greatest honor the Bible gives him was the fact that Jesus was his physical descendant who fulfilled the promise God gave through the prophet Nathan that He would sit on the throne of David forever.

As we look at the qualities of greatness in David's life, none is more important than the one that provided the greatest contrast between him and the man he succeeded on the throne—King Saul.

In 1 Samuel 15:1–3, God commanded King Saul to go into battle and destroy the Amalekites. Later, in that same chapter, the prophet Samuel confronted King Saul because, though he defeated this enemy, Saul did not destroy them. He did only a portion of what God ordered him to do. Saul's disobedience was grievous to God and His prophet: "Now the word of the Lord came to Samuel, saying, 'I greatly regret that I have set up Saul *as* king, for he has turned back from following Me, and has not performed My commandments.' And it grieved Samuel, and he cried out to the Lord all night" (vv. 10–11).

The next day, Samuel told the Saul that, because of his disobedience, the Lord repented of having made him king and was giving the kingdom to another.

> So Samuel said:
> "Has the Lord as *great* delight in burnt offerings and sacrifices,
> As in obeying the voice of the Lord?
> Behold, to obey is better than sacrifice,
> And to heed than the fat of rams.
> For rebellion *is as* the sin of witchcraft,
> And stubbornness *is as* iniquity and idolatry.
> Because you have rejected the word of the Lord,
> He also has rejected you from *being* king."
>
> Then Saul said to Samuel, "I have sinned, for I have transgressed the commandment of the Lord and your words, because I feared the people and obeyed their voice. Now therefore, please pardon my sin, and return with me, that I may worship the Lord."
>
> But Samuel said to Saul, "I will not return with you, for you have rejected the word of the Lord, and the Lord has rejected you from being king over Israel."
>
> And as Samuel turned around to go away, *Saul* seized the edge of his robe, and it tore. So Samuel said to him, "The Lord has torn the kingdom of Israel from you today, and has given it to a neighbor of yours, *who is* better than you. And also the Strength of Israel will not lie nor relent. For He *is* not a man, that He should relent" (1 Samuel 15:22–29).

So as we read the story of David's defeat of Goliath and being received into the king's court, we should remember that at this time David had been anointed to be king but had not yet been elevated to that position.

He was a king in waiting.

THE IMPORTANCE OF SUBMISSION

Have you ever had to wait for a promise of God to be fulfilled in your life? Those can be uncomfortable times—remaining faithful to the word God has given you while waiting for it to come to pass. And David received a double dose of life-threatening discomfort. First Samuel 18 tells how King Saul became jealous when the heart of the nation turned to David. The most popular songs of the day had flattering lyrics about David. In a jealous rage, Saul began a prolonged campaign of persecution against David, even trying to take the young hero's life.

During this time, David demonstrated one of the most important lessons of true greatness. In the area of submission to authority, David conducted himself flawlessly. Though he was fleeing for his life, David still honored the king who was trying to kill him. In situation after situation, David submitted himself perfectly to the authority of King Saul. He never rebelled. He never acted unrighteously. He never retaliated or sought revenge. In that submission to authority, David displayed the sixth lesson about greatness: every great person is exalted by God as he or she humbly submits to God's direct authority and to His delegated human authority on earth.

This scriptural truth has no exception. David is one example, but Jesus is the perfect example. Ordered by His mother to leave the Temple when He wanted to stay as a 12-year-old entering manhood, Jesus, the Son of God, nevertheless submitted Himself to His parents:

155

When they saw Him, they were amazed; and His mother said to Him, "Son, why have You done this to us? Look, Your father and I have sought You anxiously."

And He said to them, "Why did you seek Me? Did you not know that I must be about My Father's business?" But they did not understand the statement which He spoke to them.

Then He went down with them and came to Nazareth, and was subject to them, but His mother kept all these things in her heart. And Jesus increased in wisdom and stature, and in favor with God and men (Luke 2:48–52).

Jesus' entire ministry was based on the principle of submission. John 12:49 says, "I have not spoken on My own *authority*; but the Father who sent Me gave Me a command, what I should say and what I should speak."

John 14:10 asks, "Do you not believe that I am in the Father, and the Father in Me? The words that I speak to you I do not speak on My own *authority*; but the Father who dwells in Me does the works."

You can search God's Word from front to back and you simply will not find an exception to this important truth in the Bible. Just as Jesus was exalted by His Father because of His complete trust and submission (Philippians 2:5–11), so it was for David and will be for all of us. God's Kingdom is one of order and authority. The devil's kingdom is one of chaos and anarchy.

 God's Kingdom is one of order and authority. The devil's kingdom is one of chaos and anarchy.

Our true inner nature and whom we serve can be easily discerned by our attitudes about authority. To help us understand the gravity of this issue and how it applies to our lives, I will discuss seven important truths about the issue of submission to authority.

SEVEN TRUTHS ABOUT SUBMISSION

Every person who becomes great for God must be submitted to God's direct authority and His delegated authority on earth. Understanding this principle is essential to achieving our full potential in God. So let's examine seven scriptural truths concerning submission to authority.

TRUTH #1: WITHOUT AUTHORITY THERE IS CHAOS.

Because of our sin nature, a lack of authority would result in chaos. Isaiah 53:6 says it this way:

> All we like sheep have gone astray;
> We have turned, every one, to his own way;
> And the Lord has laid on Him the iniquity of us all.

Simply put, the very essence of our sin nature causes us to want to do things our own way—not God's way or anybody else's way. We want to do it *our* way. But think about the ultimate outcome of that approach to life. Any society that would function according to that principle would quickly descend into chaos because humans have a sin nature. Authority is the only thing that establishes the order necessary for us to be productive and protected.

Secular humanism seemingly has become the unofficial religion of the United States and most of the western world in the past 30–40 years. That philosophy openly opposes any type of authority. It has invaded our public schools and government with its premise that people do not have a sin nature. Secular humanism has tied the hands of school-teachers, removing their authority to establish an atmosphere of order to teach children. Little more than a generation ago, students held a healthy respect for principals and teachers, and if a child was disciplined at school, he knew his parents would back up the school authorities. Now, parents are more likely to side with the child and file a lawsuit against the school.

Police officers, too, have been affected by this lack of respect for authority. They are forced to jump through a thousand legal hoops just to restrain criminal activity. If the slightest thing goes wrong, the criminal is released, and the officer is chastised or even prosecuted. I've even seen bumper stickers that say, "Distrust All Authority."

Interestingly enough, the Founding Fathers of the United States had no confusion at all about this fundamental reality. They understood that we have a sin nature, so they created a criminal justice system based on the Ten Commandments and other biblical principles. It is shockingly ironic that some humanistic Supreme Court justices have made recent rulings in a chamber that still has the Ten Commandments displayed on its walls.

Because lawmakers have failed to understand what our Founding Fathers saw so clearly, our society has reaped chaos in our schools and on our streets. By refusing to acknowledge our rebellious sin nature, we lose the ability to restrain sin. Refusing to trust authority, we choose to invite disrespect and chaos.

This mindset has even brought confusion to the Church about the issue of authority. For instance, in a friendly argument, a young man suggested to one pastor of a church I served that there should be no human authority in the government of God's church—no senior pastor, no leaders, no one in charge. He recommended that the congregation meet together and let the Holy Spirit lead. He believed God then would raise up a leader for each service. This was a fine young man with no ill intent, but his suggestion revealed what must be called blatant naiveté.

Authority is what restrains our sin nature. Even in the best group of people, chaos will break out without authority. We need a president for the country, governors for the states, mayors for the cities, senior pastors for the churches, and leaders in the homes. We need leadership with authority.

TRUTH #2: ALL AUTHORITY ORIGINATES IN GOD.

The second truth about authority is this: God is the originator of authority, and Satan is the originator of rebellion. Romans 13:1 says, "Let every soul be subject to the governing authorities. For there is no authority except from God."

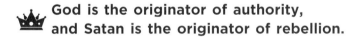 **God is the originator of authority, and Satan is the originator of rebellion.**

In our natural minds, when we read, "There is no authority except from God," we may take exception to that statement when we think in terms of specific people in leadership rather than the *position*.

To get a better grasp on this point, consider King Saul as an example. After he disobeyed God's instruction, Saul, the man, was no longer from or under God—the Spirit of God departed from him. Though he had been anointed king and he knew God, the Lord was not pleased with him. Nevertheless, David continued to be under submission to the king because he honored the *position* of authority King Saul held. When a young man came to David and said, "I killed Saul," David's response was "How was it you were not afraid to put forth your hand to destroy the Lord's anointed?" Then David ordered the young man killed on the spot. Why? Because that man had attacked not just the *man*, King Saul, but also the *position* Saul held by God's direct appointment (2 Samuel 1:1–17).

God appoints the positions of authority that exist to fulfill His purposes. Therefore, anyone who resists that authority resists the ordinance of God. Paul says, "Rulers are not a terror to good works, but to evil. Do you want to be unafraid of the authority? Do what is good, and you will have praise from the same" (Romans 13:3).

According to the Bible, the person in authority is God's minister to us. This truth is repeated three times in Romans 13 (verses 4 and 6). But how does authority minister to us? By restraining our sin nature and that of the people around us. After all, sin nature without restraint would be harmful. Traffic rules are an example of this principle. Traffic signs and speed limits may at times annoy us. We may want to drive faster than the posted speed limit, or we may not want to obey all the traffic rules. But what if every driver had his own way? We really should be thankful there are not only rules but also police officers to enforce them, especially when newly licensed, 16-year-old boys full of testosterone want to speed and are searching for thrills. In fact, most of us thought we were bullet proof until we got into our late 20s.

When my brother Randy turned 16, he was a football player and thought he was something special. He raced his 1957 Chevrolet up and down our street as fast as he could go. Also living on our street was a mentally challenged young boy who rode his bicycle up and down the street from morning until evening. We would greet the friendly young man as he pedaled by and waved to us. His father, on the other hand, was a fearsome man. He was a mechanic who had been a boxer in the Navy.

One day, the boy was riding down the street as Randy came racing up the street. My brother pulled into our driveway, and the boy's dad was right behind him. "The next time you drive down the street that fast," the father said, "I'm going to take the wheels off your car." My brother respectfully said, "Okay!" That was all it took to restrain Randy for the sake of that young boy.

Authority ministers to us. It helps restrain our sin nature and the sin nature of people who could potentially cause harm to everyone. Authority is a good thing! Those who do good do not need to be afraid of authority. The fear belongs to those who do evil.

Let's take a little more in-depth look at what Paul tells us about the role of God-given authority:

> He is God's minister to you for good. But if you do evil, be afraid; for he does not bear the sword in vain; for he is God's minister, an avenger to *execute* wrath on him who practices evil. Therefore *you* must be subject, not only because of wrath but also for conscience' sake. For because of this you also pay taxes, for they are God's ministers attending continually to this very thing. Render therefore to all their due: taxes to whom taxes *are due*, customs to whom customs, fear to whom fear, honor to whom honor (Romans 13:4–7).

When human authority corrects us, it is God correcting us. Notice the term Paul uses here. He calls human authority "God's ministers." The role of that minister is as "an avenger to execute wrath on him who does evil." That is why we are to honor and be subject to authority; not only out of fear but also out of a good conscience. Paying our taxes not out of constraint but out of respect, and honoring those positions of authority with our words and actions instead of belittling or cursing them. Authority is a minister of God to correct us when we're doing something wrong, to restrain our sin nature, and to cause us to pay taxes. Why do we pay taxes? So there will be ministers up and down the street restraining our sin nature—so there will be governing authorities that can bring order into our society and prevent chaos from breaking out.

Properly honoring and supporting authority is central to the fulfillment of God's plans and purposes in our lives, individually and corporately. To see just how vital it is, look at 2 Thessalonians 2:7–9:

> The mystery of lawlessness is already at work; only He who now restrains *will do so* until He is taken out of the way. And then the lawless one will be revealed, whom the Lord will consume with the breath of His mouth and destroy with the brightness of His coming. The coming of the *lawless one* is according to the working of Satan.

We have all heard the term "Antichrist" used, especially in the context of the end times. But here we see another name for him—"the lawless one." The lawless one, the Antichrist, is the embodiment of Satan himself. His coming is according to the working of Satan. Satan is the god of lawlessness. One of the indications that we are living in the end times is the exponential growth of lawlessness on the earth—a worldwide spirit of anarchy and rebellion.

It is easy to see that wherever lawlessness takes hold, Satan exists. Satan works in an atmosphere of rebellion, and God only works in an atmosphere of order and submission.

Remember how Jesus told us to pray:

Your kingdom come.
Your will be done
On earth as *it is* in heaven (Matthew 6:10).

The word translated "kingdom" here is the Greek word meaning "direct rule." So we could translate that phrase as "Let Your *direct rule* come and let Your will be done just as it is in heaven."

How are things done in heaven? Heaven is a place of perfect order. There's been only one rebellion in heaven, and it was dealt with decisively. That was the day Lucifer stood up as the light bearer and a worshipper of God, according to Isaiah 14 and Ezekiel 28, and rebelled against the Lord. So persuasive was his deception that Lucifer took a third of the angels in heaven with him when God threw him out.

God will not tolerate rebellion. That is just the way heaven operates. So when we pray the Lord's Prayer, what we are praying is "God, I want there to be order and submission in my life just as it would be done in heaven."

Then notice the next thing Jesus instructs us to pray: "Give us this day our daily bread" (v. 11). Once you have submitted, anything God has is yours. Once you're submitted to God and to authority, you can pray the rest of that prayer. But you cannot skip "Your kingdom come. Your will be done on earth as it is in heaven" and expect to receive the rest of the promises in that prayer. Submission to authority opens God's heart and hand to us as we walk in His will.

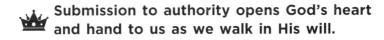 **Submission to authority opens God's heart and hand to us as we walk in His will.**

TRUTH #3: THE CONSEQUENCES OF REBELLION ARE SERIOUS.

Since all authority comes from God, the third truth about submission to authority should be no surprise: Rebellion against God's direct or delegated human authority is a serious sin with serious consequences. It's not cute or charming. We should not be proud of having a "free spirit," nor should we justify it in others.

In our current society, many role models for young people, and even older people, are rebels—musicians, athletes, and movie stars. A great percentage of these celebrities are blatantly rebellious toward authority. By some standards, such an attitude makes them notable personalities—more marketable. The Bible never says rebellion is worthy of admiration, though. Instead, it calls it serious sin: "Whoever resists the authority resists the ordinance of God, and those who resist will bring judgment on themselves" (Romans 13:2).

Look again at what Samuel said when he confronted King Saul for his rebellion:

> Has the Lord *as great* delight in burnt offerings and sacrifices,
> As in obeying the voice of the Lord?
> Behold, to obey is better than sacrifice,
> *And* to heed than the fat of rams (1 Samuel 15:22).

Saul was trying to justify his rebellion by pointing out that he had offered a sacrifice to the Lord from some of the spoil. However, God had ordered him to destroy that livestock. Samuel responded by basically saying, "You can't buy off God." That is just as true today. It doesn't matter how much money we drop in the offering container or anything else we might say we do for Him—nothing will substitute for obedience. We cannot justify ourselves.

Just how grievous is rebellion against God? Samuel goes on to say,

> For rebellion *is as* the sin of witchcraft,
> And stubbornness *is as* iniquity and idolatry.
> Because you have rejected the word of the Lord,
> He also has rejected you from *being* king (v. 23).

Witchcraft is an abomination to the Lord. Understand that witchcraft is basically using our own abilities to create our own results—effectively becoming our own gods. It's an attitude that says, *I want a husband, a wife, another job. I'm going to come up with a potion, a motion, or a notion to get what I want. I'm going to use my own spirit and my own abilities to get my own way. I don't need God. I'm going to find a way to make it happen.* This is exactly the way God defines rebellion—trying to create results our way rather than coming to Him. It is not cute. It is an abomination. And it cannot be excused.

In the same way Samuel equated rebellion with witchcraft, so he also equated stubbornness with iniquity and idolatry. Idolatry means exalting another god above the one true God. You may wonder, "Why would he say stubbornness is like idolatry?"

The reason is that stubbornness is the worship of my own opinion. Here is what happens: I ignore what God tells me to do because I believe my own ideas are better than His. I will even idolize my opinion and exalt it above God's Word and the will of those God placed in authority over me. Therefore, if you disagree with my opinion, I'm going to resist you openly and secretly. When someone in authority tells me to do something I don't want to do, I'm going to resist and argue or oppose them in secret. And if I eventually do what I am told, I'll act like a stubborn old mule that has to be dragged every step of the way because my own opinion has become my god.

God says that when He sees rebellion it is equivalent to the sin of witchcraft. When He sees stubbornness toward authority, it's just like the sin of idolatry. This matter is serious to God. Rebellion and stubbornness will cut you off from the blessings God wants to pour out on you. James 4 says,

> "God resists the proud,
> But gives grace to the humble."
> Therefore submit to God. Resist the devil and he will flee
>   from you (vv. 6–7; see also 1 Peter 5:5–6).

> ### Rebellion and stubbornness will cut you off from the blessings God wants to pour out on you.

Yes, God extends grace to imperfect people. But the condition for receiving that grace is humility displayed in submission. The proud will not submit, so God resists them. The humble will submit, so God gives them grace and blessings.

The word translated "resist" means 'to set in battle formation.' When someone is too proud to submit, God will set Himself in battle array against such a person. There is no way for this person to succeed because God can't be defeated. If you are in rebellion to authority on any level, then you are in rebellion against God, and He will resist you even though He loves you and is totally for you. He is a God of grace and mercy, which is good news for all of us. However, He is also a

God of authority. Your refusal to honor authority will cut you off from the flow of His grace.

Rebellion leaves us without spiritual protection. Notice the order in James 4:6. First, it says we are to submit to God. Then we should resist the devil and he will flee from us. We can't resist the devil until we have submitted to God. When we are in rebellion, the devil has access to us, and his mission is to steal, kill, and destroy. We can cry and pray all we want, but it won't matter. We'll still be in deep trouble until we repent and submit to God. It's not because God doesn't like us or want to help us. No, He loves us more than anyone else does and He is graciously willing and waiting to help us. It is simply a matter of the position we have taken by choice.

To give you a better understanding of this concept, think about what parents do when adolescent children go through times of rebellion. In those years, I told our children, "If you want to do the right thing, you're looking at your best friend. If you want to do the wrong thing, you're looking at your worst enemy. I'll fight you every step of the way if you are trying to destroy yourself. If you're telling me that you want to drink, take drugs, or rebel in some way, I'll oppose you. But if you're telling me that you need my support for music lessons, athletics, education, or things that will help you succeed, I will do anything I can to help. I will be your best friend."

God loves you more than any other person loves you. He created you in your mother's womb for a wonderful purpose. When you are acting in pride and rebellion, He is not rejecting you. He is resisting the pride and rebellion in you that originates from hell itself. God resists pride because He has your best interests at heart. His response is not out of anger, hate, rejection, or not believing in you. It is a response of love.

Love is willing to fight you when you are going the wrong direction. It does not pat you on the back while you are on your way to hell. When I am in error, I want somebody to get in front of me and say, "Stop! You're going the wrong way, Jimmy. I love you. Now stop!" That's what God does—He opposes the proud. Why? To get us to do things His way—the way that allows Him to release the blessings of His grace that assure our success in His plan for our destiny.

> **Love is willing to fight you when you are going the wrong direction.**

TRUTH #4: SALVATION REQUIRES SUBMISSION.

The fourth truth about submission to authority is that it is the condition of salvation—the thing that distinguishes the righteous from the unrighteous. The apostle Paul says,

> What does it [Scripture] say? "The word is near you, in your mouth and in your heart" (that is, the word of faith which we preach): that if you confess with your mouth the Lord Jesus and believe in your heart that God has raised Him from the dead, you will be saved. For with the heart one believes unto righteousness, and with the mouth confession is made unto salvation (Romans 10:8–10).

The confession given here for salvation is not "Jesus Christ." It is not "Jesus is Savior." It is "Jesus is Lord." Salvation begins with the repentance (turning away) from rebellion: "Jesus, I come to You. I've gone my own way, and that is the essence of sin. Because of that, God laid the penalty for my iniquity on You. So I come to receive Your forgiveness for rebelling—for going my own way. With my mouth I openly confess You as my Lord, and I surrender my life and submit to You."

Some people say they believe Jesus is the Son of God. They might even believe that He died for their sins. However, until they have laid down their authority over their own lives and given them to Jesus, I question whether they are saved. When we are truly converted (completely changed), the Bible says we have become "a new creation; old things have passed away; behold, all things have become new" (2 Corinthians 5:17). One of the most obvious signs that a person has become a believer is a dramatically different attitude toward authority.

In Jericho, Jesus told a story about a nobleman giving each of his ten servants the same amount of money to manage while he was gone. Later, some men in the kingdom sent a delegation telling him that they would no longer be ruled by him. On his return, he first addressed the servants. One of the servants had earned 10 times the value of what he was given, and another earned 5 times what he had been given. The nobleman deemed these two servants faithful and promoted them as rulers over 10 cities and 5 cities, respectively.

But one servant did nothing with the money except bury it in the ground. He then offered this excuse: "I feared you, because you are an austere man. You collect what you did not deposit, and reap what you did not sow" (Luke 19:21). The nobleman's "reward" to him was ironically the very thing this servant had said. The nobleman responded, "Out of your own mouth I will judge you, *you* wicked servant. You knew that I was an austere man, collecting what I did not deposit and reaping what I did not sow. Why then did you not put my money in the bank, that at my coming I might have collected it with interest?" (vv. 22–23). The nobleman then took what he had given this man and turned around to give it to the man who had multiplied his portion 10 times. Finally, the nobleman ordered for the men who had rebelled against his authority to be summoned and executed: "Bring here those enemies of mine, who did not want me to reign over them, and slay *them* before me" (v. 27).

If you've never submitted your life to God and made Him the Lord of your life, then you have yet to meet the primary condition of salvation. "If you confess with your mouth the Lord Jesus" means you have made the decision to no longer be lord of your life—you are not qualified to run it, have not done a good job trying, realize it is the wrong way, and give total control of your life to God.

Salvation does not mean you are perfect or that you will never make another mistake. It does require you to recognize God as the ruler of your life to whom you freely give yourself as a servant. One of the most obvious distinctions between Christians and those who are not should be an attitude of submission to authority and a humility that accepts the fact that someone is reigning over us.

> **If you've never submitted your life to God and made Him the Lord of your life, then you have yet to meet the primary condition of salvation.**

TRUTH #5: WE GAIN AUTHORITY THROUGH SUBMISSION.

We can also see in Jesus' parable about the faithful servants the fifth truth about authority and submission: In God's kingdom, you can have only as much authority as you are under, both natural and spiritual.

In the military, no intelligent high-ranking officer is going to entrust a weapon to someone who is not submitted to authority. The more submitted and capable you are, the more authority you will be given.

Jesus explained how He was submitted to the Father's authority: "The Son can do nothing of Himself, but what

He sees the Father do; for whatever He does, the Son also does in like manner" (John 5:19). The greatest miracles in the world were done by the man who was most submitted to authority in the history of the world. Jesus submitted to His parents and to God. He did not consider Himself His own. Jesus openly admitted, "I only do what I see My Father do."

Two other submitted men in the Bible were Joseph and Daniel. Both rose from slavery to assume incredible regulatory powers in the nations that held them captive. Both men were totally submitted to human kings, even though those rulers did not believe in the God of Israel. Daniel, when told to do something that would violate the authority of God in his life, handled the situation with a submitted heart. He showed respect for the king's position and recognized the authority of the king's order. As the king's subject, he humbly submitted himself to the consequences of violating those orders. Yet both Joseph and Daniel were exalted.

Many people try to claw their way to the top, but the best way you can get there is to bow your way to the top. "Humble yourselves in the sight of the Lord," James 4:10 says, "and He will lift you up."

In my roles as senior pastor of a church and as CEO of MarriageToday, I have promoted many people. My top consideration in promotion is the person's humility and submission. I'm always looking for good people to promote. Giftedness is less important to me than attitude. All people are gifted, but only the ones who are humble and submitted have the capacity to work for and with others to build a successful organization.

Understand that God is the one who promotes, not people. You may be tempted to say, "I'll never get ahead with my boss. I know my boss will never promote me." But you don't need your boss promoting you when God promotes you. In fact, submission to your boss will get you promoted by God. God is only going to give you as much authority as you are under.

This is just as true in the spiritual realm. Maybe you've said "I have this vision of healing people. I have this vision of preaching to nations." Remember, God will release to you only as much spiritual authority as you willingly place yourself under. God is a genius—a military genius. He understands that He cannot put a weapon in your hands that has any power when you are not submitted.

For 30 years, I have believed and operated in the spiritual gifts. I have seen wonders, miracles, and blessings happen. I believe in the power of the Holy Spirit. But I have seen people who call themselves believers use spiritual gifts to curse each other, hurt each other, and seek self-promotion in wicked ways. When you're not submitted, God cannot trust you, and He will not give you His authority. But when you're submitted, God will give you as much authority as you will recognize.

TRUTH #6: SUBMISSION ACCELERATES SPIRITUALITY.

As you understand and accept the principle of submission to authority it will accelerate your maturity and access to spiritual revelation. This sixth truth of submission to authority is clearly seen in the story of Jesus' encounter with the Roman army officer:

> When Jesus had entered Capernaum, a centurion came to Him, pleading with Him, saying, "Lord, my servant is lying at home paralyzed, dreadfully tormented."
> And Jesus said to him, "I will come and heal him."
> The centurion answered and said, "Lord, I am not worthy that You should come under my roof. But only

speak a word, and my servant will be healed. For I also am a man under authority, having soldiers under me. And I say to this *one*, 'Go,' and he goes; and to another, 'Come,' and he comes; and to my servant, 'Do this,' and he does *it*."

When Jesus heard *it*, He marveled, and said to those who followed, "Assuredly, I say to you, I have not found such great faith, not even in Israel!" (Matthew 8:5–10).

Can you imagine having faith that would cause Jesus to marvel? That was true of this non-Jewish military officer from a foreign occupation army. Notice, the issue was not this man's faith for healing. It was his understanding of and respect for authority. "I understand authority, for I am also under authority and daily issue commands to those in authority under me," the centurion said. "Because I recognize the power of the authority You operate under, I know You don't need to come to my house for my servant to be healed. All You need to do is speak the command, and it will be done." And Jesus said of this non-Israelite, "He is the most faith-filled person I've found in all of Israel." At that time, in Israel, the Jews were an occupied nation in a constant state of rebellion and opposition to Roman authority. It took a Roman centurion, a man who understood the authority of Caesar and submitted to that authority, to declare this powerful spiritual truth.

Submission to authority is an indispensable interpretive key to the Bible. If you don't understand this principle, you will not understand other foundational spiritual principles. The Bible is a book about the kingdom of God—whose King who will not tolerate rebellion. Until you understand submission to authority, the Bible will remain a clouded book to you. But when you understand the kingdom of God and the way God operates, suddenly you will find yourself opening the Bible and saying, "Oh yes!" You will understand why some people who have been believers for two or three years have grown so fast in the Lord, while others who have been believers for 40 or 50 years are spiritual infants because they have never submitted to authority or understood the concept.

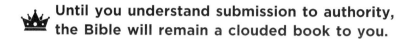
Until you understand submission to authority, the Bible will remain a clouded book to you.

TRUTH #7: SUBMISSION BRINGS SUPERNATURAL FAVOR.

The seventh truth about submission to authority is that it brings God's supernatural favor, blessing, and protection. This principle is at work in Ephesians 6:1–3: "Children, obey your parents in the Lord, for this is right. 'Honor your father and mother,' which is the first commandment with promise: 'that it may be well with you and you may live long on the earth.'"

Some mothers and fathers think it's "modern parenting" to allow their children to rebel and do their own thing. They believe their children will ultimately find their own way and grow out of rebellion and foolishness. But if you want to be a good parent, you must understand this: if you don't teach your children to obey, you are cursing them.

I am not saying parental authority should be unloving or without true relationship. You can't shout commands at your children all of the time and expect good results. For your discipline to be effective and your authority to be respected, you must be affectionate with your children and show them lots of personal attention. You also need to be verbally affectionate and continually tell them how much you believe in them. Parental authority must be relational in order to be effective.

You earn the right to discipline your children by how you show them love. Your authority must be relational. Also, you must teach your children to obey and honor you, because that is "the first commandment with promise: 'that it may be well with you and you may live long on the earth.'"

Remember, you are the first of many authority figures in your children's lives. If you don't teach them to respect your authority, then they will carry that same disrespect to other authority figures. They will have ongoing problems relating to authority. As parents, we must acknowledge that for the rest of their lives our children will constantly deal with human authority, which will either bless or curse them—depending on their response.

In John 14:21, Jesus says, "He who has My commandments and keeps them, it is he who loves Me. And he who loves Me will be loved by My Father, and I will love him and manifest Myself to him." Consider what is at stake over the issue of willing obedience to authority: Jesus manifesting Himself to us by revelation through His Word.

Then Jesus says, "If anyone loves Me, he will keep My word; and My Father will love him, and We will come to him and make Our home with him" (v. 23). Relationship with God doesn't get any more intimate than that—having our heavenly Father and His Son living in us! This Bible passage doesn't mean God doesn't love people who aren't submitted. It simply means God doesn't express His love to them in the same, intimate way.

As parents, Karen and I saw this principle at work. We always loved our son and daughter. When they were growing up, there was not a minute we didn't love them. Nevertheless, there were times when we could not give them the affection we wanted to show them. Even though we felt the same love, in those times we needed to express it through discipline. We always wanted to pull them up in our arms and hug and kiss them and tell them how much we loved them, but sometimes their behavior would not allow us to show our love in that way.

Jesus does not want to discipline us for the rest of our lives. He wants us to grow into His likeness so we will practice self-discipline. But He will discipline, if necessary, because of His love for us. He is calling us to a point of maturity where we will say, "I'm not qualified to run my life. So, Lord, I submit myself. I humble myself and I admit how much I need You. I confess You as the Lord of my life. I also realize the delegated human authorities around me are Your ministers. They are set in place to help restrain my sin nature and the sin nature of those around me. Rather than going through my life resisting You and resisting authority, Lord, I submit right now."

That is what a mature person under authority does. And that's what David did.

Part Six

THE WISE LEADER

Lesson 7

ADMIT WEAKNESSES
AND BECOME ACCOUNTABLE
TO OTHERS

THOSE WHO DESIRE the greatness God intends for their lives share a common outcome—they become leaders. When they accept and pursue greatness on God's terms, these great people become the leaders God called them to be within their own families. Then God calls them to step into roles of leadership in every area of life—in their workplaces, churches, civic organizations, governmental institutions, and so on. As they assume their God-given positions, God uses these people to bring His way of thinking and acting into every corner of society. You may discover you have a full-time calling and anointing for leadership. Your destiny may be as a leader in business, or perhaps your area of interest and anointing is found in ministry, medicine, education, athletics, entertainment, or something else.

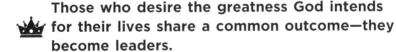 **Those who desire the greatness God intends for their lives share a common outcome—they become leaders.**

Regardless of the arena into which God called you, I want to warn you of an inward struggle you will experience related to your own ability to assume leadership. Invariably, questions such as these will flood your thoughts: *Just who do you think you are? You know the areas of weakness in your life, so what makes you think you're qualified to accept God's call to a higher level of leadership?* Does this sound familiar? Self-doubt is a nearly universal human experience. When the Bible tells a story, it tells the *whole* story. Not only does it include good things about a person but also the bad.

The Bible's account of David's life exemplifies this truth. Though David was undoubtedly one of the greatest leaders in history who displayed many exceptional qualities, the Bible does not account his success to the idea that he was perfect. Rather, it shows that David was an extraordinary leader *in spite of* all his shortcomings.

Scripture shines a spotlight on all of his awesome qualities and incredible accomplishments, but it also exposes some glaring weaknesses and problems. It tells the story of a man who with God's help defeated Goliath against overwhelming odds. But it also tells the sordid story of David and Bathsheba. It reveals how, later in life, David tried to establish his own greatness by counting the population and soldiers under his command. In recounting his conflicts and difficulties with Absalom, the Bible portrays David as a poor father. This great leader had some obvious problems and inconsistencies in his life. So how could David become so great in spite of all his weaknesses? The Bible gives us the answer and it can forever settle the question in our own minds.

WHOSE DO YOU THINK YOU ARE?

David was an extraordinary leader despite his human weaknesses. The same is true for you and me. God created each of us with a call of greatness on our lives. No doubt, while we may recognize our areas of gifting, at the same time we also recognize areas in our lives that are a mess. No one is without problems, and we need to be honest about it.

God created each of us with a call of greatness on our lives.

The question we need to ask is this: *how do we achieve greatness in spite of our weaknesses?* David achieved greatness, not only because of the way he used his strengths, but also because of how he dealt with his weaknesses. The first thing he did with his shortcomings was admit them! He was transparent and honest before God. He also surrounded himself with godly people who could strengthen and add to his life while holding him accountable for his actions. I believe accountability was the secret of David's success as a leader and a distinction that set him apart from every other king of Israel.

It's important to recognize that what we do with our weaknesses has as much bearing on our future success as what we do with our strengths. Yes, any leader—whether in business, ministry, or any other field—must hone his or her natural abilities and develop them into something great. That is simply good stewardship of the giftings and skills God has given to each of us. However, just as important is taking responsibility for the areas in which we lack strength.

It is vital for us to recognize, appreciate, and develop our gifts. But it is just as important for us to acknowledge that our giftings are isolated, and we are weak in some areas. If we are in touch with reality, we know we have weaknesses and problems. But does that mean we give up and give in to failure? Do we walk away in shame? *No.*

As gifted as we may be, and as many strengths as we may possess, all of us are all totally inadequate *on our own* to accomplish what God has called us to do. David certainly knew that fact. So he surrounded himself with God and godly people who were gifted and strong where he wasn't. That is the only reason he survived and accomplished all that he did.

TRANSPARENCY AND HUMILITY

The book of Psalms highlights David's transparency. For instance, the title of Psalm 51 is "To the Chief Musician. A Psalm of David when Nathan the prophet went to him, after he had gone in to Bathsheba." This Psalm verifies the record of David's adultery with Bathsheba and how Nathan the prophet rebuked him.

Elsewhere, Psalm 18 is entitled "To the Chief Musician. A Psalm of David the servant of the Lord, who spoke to the Lord the words of this song on the day that the Lord delivered him from the hand of all his enemies and from the hand of Saul." David begins with this declaration:

> I will love You, O Lord, my strength.
> The Lord is my rock and my fortress and my deliverer;
> My God, my strength, in whom I will trust;
> My shield and the horn of my salvation, my stronghold.
> I will call upon the Lord, who is worthy to be praised;
> So shall I be saved from my enemies.
> The pangs of death surrounded me,
> And the floods of ungodliness made me afraid (Psalm 18:1–4).

This is an open admission of fear from the same man who killed Goliath armed only with a slingshot and a few stones. Yes, David confesses his fear *without shame.* This disclosure is not easy for most of us.

Then David continues:
The sorrows of Sheol surrounded me;
The snares of death confronted me....
The Lord thundered from heaven,
And the Most High uttered His voice,
Hailstones and coals of fire.
He sent out His arrows and scattered the foe,
Lightnings in abundance, and He vanquished them.
Then the channels of the sea were seen,
The foundations of the world were uncovered
At Your rebuke, O Lord,
At the blast of the breath of Your nostrils.
He sent from above, He took me;
He drew me out of many waters.
He delivered me from my strong enemy,
From those who hated me,
For they were too strong for me.
They confronted me in the day of my calamity,
But the Lord was my support (Psalm 18:5, 13–18).

David confesses his fear
without shame.

This Psalm shows why David was a man after God's heart. It was because David was an honest man—a man without guile, a man who did not pretend to be strong when he wasn't. He was not a man who hid behind his accomplishments, nor did he hide behind his problems, failures, and fears. David openly admitted it all and said, "God, You're my refuge and my strength. You're my fortress. I trust in You. I'm afraid these people are too strong for me."

God responded by protecting David and then exalted him as the king who would establish the throne for Jesus to sit upon. As we read this psalm written by David, we are reading the record of a man who acknowledged his weaknesses and turned to God for help.

Where were the songs of Saul, the king who preceded David? According to the Bible's description, he had just as much, and perhaps even more, natural ability than David. Saul, too, was anointed by God for leadership. *Where are his psalms?* Yet King Saul had no songs. He was a man filled with pride. He was a man God rejected as a leader because Saul did not take his weaknesses and give them to God. Saul did not surround himself with good men who could help him in the areas where he was not gifted. He was an arrogant man who tried to handle things on his own, which ultimately led to his rejection as king. When Saul chose to solve a problem his own way, rather than God's way, God said, "I regret that I ever made Saul king." Saul had no humility and no transparency. No wonder he had no psalms.

Let me ask you a question: Do you have any psalms? Could you write honestly before God? The history of a life is the record of a person. If you had to sit down right now and recount the way you dealt with your problems in your past, would it be a psalm declaring your need for God and testifying of the ways He has helped you? Would it be a record like Psalm 18 was for David: an open admission of your weaknesses, problems, and fears and your decision to turn everything over to God? Or would you be ashamed of your weaknesses? Have you tried to hide them? Have you handled everything on your own? In areas of insecurity, inadequacy, and mistakes, have you chosen to protect and isolate yourself in hope that no one will think you have any problems?

Learning to embrace your weaknesses is the first essential step on the journey to becoming great and ascending into leadership. You must learn to become honest about who you are and who you are not. Then you must surround yourself with relationships and accountability. Leaders are open about their weaknesses and surround themselves with God and godly people. It works that way every time.

The opposite is also true. People who chronically fall short of their destinies in God are prideful, insecure, and unwilling to admit their weaknesses. They avoid becoming accountable and fail to develop close connections with godly people.

David refused to hide from his weaknesses or to conceal those weaknesses from those around him. He knew his strength came from a Source outside of himself. David knew his life was enhanced by those he drew in close beside him.

ADMITTING WEAKNESSES

David embraced the seventh truth about greatness: every great person is incomplete in his or her giftings, personality, and intellect. **Only through an honest admission of those weaknesses and the help and accountability of others can a person ascend to greatness and remain there.**

By now, you have seen that the greatness God has designed us for is quite different from greatness as the world and the secular media present it. Greatness God's way is not accomplished through our own efforts. It will not manifest itself in a vacuum. And it does not reach its highest point when people make it appear they have attained success apart from the help of God and others. Every wise leader knows this about true greatness in leadership: *We cannot reach greatness alone. We have all been divinely disabled.*

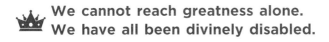 **We cannot reach greatness alone. We have all been divinely disabled.**

How did Moses respond when God called him to leadership and told him to deliver the children of Israel from Egypt? "But I can't talk," he said. And he was right. God didn't argue with him. Instead, God said, "Who made your mouth, Moses?" What about the apostle Paul When he showed up in churches to preach, he said he was unimpressive in speech. He was a brilliant writer but not a great speaker—a fact for which people criticized him. Paul openly admitted his weakness. Moses and Paul were divinely disabled—they knew they couldn't do it alone.

What is your limitation, area of weakness, or need? The fact is, God has disabled every one of us in one way or another. He has done this so we will learn to depend on Him and other people. If you come across someone who pretends to have it all together, then you are meeting a deceived or insecure individual. No one gets the whole package. That doesn't mean, though, that we should back down from our destiny, which includes excellence or influence, just because we don't have every quality and ability for a particular task. When we depend on God and each other, we've got the whole package!

FIVE AREAS OF DEPENDENCE

David knew he had to depend on God in his weakness. The king established five areas of dependence that enabled him to be a wise and great leader, and these same five areas of dependence will help you ascend to greatness and become successful.

DEPENDENCY #1: GOD

The book of Psalms records David's dependence on God. For example, in Psalm 23:1, David writes,

> The Lord *is* my shepherd;
> I shall not want.

David saw himself as a sheep and God as the Shepherd. Having been a shepherd, he knew that sheep are totally dependent upon the shepherd. So, after declaring that the Lord was his Shepherd, David set forth in the rest of Psalm 23 a list of everything God did for him. This list illustrates his total dependence upon God.

If we are walking with God, we will have psalms in our lives. Our psalms are written in our prayer lives and our praise lives. Our dependence upon God will rise no higher than our prayer lives. I don't pray less because I have reached certain goals in my life. No, at this point in our spiritual lives, Karen and I pray a lot—in many ways, more than ever. But developing that transparent communication with our heavenly Father about our need for Him was not easy. I, for one, struggled for many years to develop a regular time of fellowship with Him. When I first became a Christian, someone told me that I should pray for an hour. So I tried to do that first thing in the morning, just as a religious ritual that I hoped would win points with God. After only two minutes, I was bored and distracted. I felt like a failure because I couldn't pray.

Today, prayer is a natural and vital part of my relationship with God. It is a part of how I express my love for Him, and it's easy. Because I'm depending on God for wisdom, strength, guidance, and provision, prayer is simply natural. I don't put a stopwatch on my prayer time—I put a calendar to it. It's every day. It's every month. It's every year. I need Him. And because I need Him, I look forward to having dialogue with Him.

The degree to which we don't pray is the degree to which we think of ourselves as independent of God. And the degree to which we do pray is the degree to which we recognize our absolute dependence on Him. God will never let you succeed without Him. But He is a willing partner and a wonderful Father for those who will admit their weaknesses and rely on Him.

DEPENDENCY #2: THE OPPOSITE SEX

David had a second level of dependence in his life in his willingness to respect and receive wisdom and insight from the opposite sex. David had more than one wife, and although that practice was not ordained by God, it was not uncommon for monarchs or wealthy men in that culture. From the Bible accounts, he listened to the counsel of his wives, which means David valued the advice of women.

For instance, he listened to the counsel of his wife Michal, Saul's daughter, at a crucial time when she said, "Dave, you have to get out of here tonight. My father is going to kill you." David did what she said and left. (See 1 Samuel 19:11–12.) First Samuel 25 tells the story of Abigail, whose husband Nabal was a foolish, hateful, and wicked man. At one point, David became so angry at Nabal that he was preparing to kill him. But Abigail, "a woman of good understanding and beautiful appearance" (v. 3), stepped in and counseled David not to do it, and he listened to her. Shortly after that, Nabal died. Then David married this woman he had listened to with respect (v. 35).

During the exile of David's rebellious son Absalom, a woman approached David hoping to prevail upon the king to bring his son home (2 Samuel 14). David listened to her. Then, on his deathbed, David listened to the counsel of Bathsheba concerning naming his successor. "You'd better do something because the nation's about to be divided," she said. Because of her counsel, David acted and settled the issue by confirming Solomon as the heir to the throne.

These Scriptures confirm that David willingly received information, advice, and counsel from women. And it saved his life and reputation. David is an example of a man who was not chauvinistic and demeaning to the opposite sex. He did not ignore their counsel. Instead, he honored and listened to them. Jesus was even more respectful to women. Good men and women are that way. Godly leaders are that way. Men and women need each other to achieve their greatest potential in God. We just simply can't get there without each other.

 Men and women need each other to achieve their greatest potential in God.

DEPENDENCY #3: GOD'S ANOINTED MINISTERS

Dependence on God's anointed ministers and other godly men is a third pillar in the foundation of David's success. His respect for and dependence upon the prophet Nathan features prominently in David's story. This prophet was his spiritual covering. Consider Nathan's confrontation of King David with the sin of adultery with Bathsheba and the arranged murder of her husband, Uriah. Nathan placed his own life in danger when he approached the king and rebuked him. Rather than coming against Nathan for exposing him, David repented. Later, on David's deathbed, the king still received counsel from the prophet. David knew the value of spiritual covering, accepted it, and responded to it. He also valued the covering of other men, such as his mighty men. David was a relationally connected person.

Being rightly connected to God's spiritual covering from other godly men and women in our lives is important. Hebrews 13:7 instructs us, "Remember those who rule over you, who have spoken the word of God to you, whose faith follow, considering the outcome of *their* conduct." Then verse 17 says, "Obey those who rule over you, and be submissive, for they watch out for your souls, as those who must give an account. Let them do so with joy and not with grief, for that would be unprofitable for you."

The apostle Paul writes in 1 Corinthians 12 about how incomplete we are individually and how much we need each other:

> The body is not one member but many.
>
> If the foot should say, "Because I am not a hand, I am not of the body," is it therefore not of the body? And if the ear should say, "Because I am not an eye, I am not of the body," is it therefore not of the body? If the whole body *were* an eye, where *would be* the hearing? If the whole *were* hearing, where *would be* the smelling? But now God has set the members, each one of them, in the body just as He pleased. And if they were all one member, where *would* the body be?
>
> But now indeed *there are* many members, yet one body. And the eye cannot say to the hand, "I have no need of you"; nor again the head to the feet, "I have no need of you" (1 Corinthians 12:14–21).

Imagine a room full of dismembered body parts trying to get anything accomplished. It would seem ridiculous—and morbid. The same is true when Christians act independently of each other and expect to achieve anything of value.

I know this for a fact. I have had some level of success in my ministry and life. But if you think I was some genius who got there because I was particularly gifted or anything like that, you would be completely wrong. It has taken thousands of people alongside me to get the job done. Thousands of people have worked in my life to help me get where I am today.

When Karen and I joined Trinity Fellowship Church in Amarillo, Texas, we submitted ourselves to the elders of the church. As we became connected to the body of the church and I realized who I was in Christ, my giftings were seen, and my ministry was released. God began taking us up one rung at a time. He is still using that principle of submission to spiritual covering and authority to continue taking us higher. But whether I am an eye, an ear, or a toenail, if I detach myself from the body of Christ, then my chances of going anywhere disappear.

Now, all of us tend toward frustration with people who aren't like us. For instance, you may be an "ear" and hear things very accurately. Perhaps you are prophetic, or you just hear God in a certain way. If you aren't careful, you will let yourself become frustrated with people who can't hear in the same way you can. Or maybe you are a foot—you like going places and getting things done, and you get disappointed that everyone else is just sitting around. What you must realize is that they may be the eye, the mouth, or the hand that you need.

We need eyes so we don't run into walls. We need mouths to voice what we are hearing. We need each other. What we don't need is to stand back and criticize each other because we're not alike. We're all different in our giftings for a purpose. Only by working together will we be able to hear, see, smell, sense, and go where God wants us to go. David purposed to be a connected man. He had a healthy dependence on his spiritual covering and the people around him who also loved and served the Lord.

DEPENDENCY #4: CLOSE FRIENDS

We all need friends. Significant in David's story is his friendship with King Saul's son Jonathan. Jonathan was a giant killer himself and a great warrior. Unlike his father, Jonathan was a great and good man. In fact, he saved David from being killed by King Saul. David trusted Jonathan and received his advice and counsel.

Proverbs 12:26 instructs,

> The righteous should choose his friends carefully,
> For the way of the wicked leads them astray.

For one thing, we should choose our friends carefully because of peer pressure. Some peer pressure is good, but some is bad. The wrong kind draws us away from God's wisdom and direction and entices us to do harmful things. When I was growing up, I experience a lot of peer pressure to drink, smoke, run around, and do bad things. The first thing God ever said to me after I got saved was "Never see your friends again."

Does being saved mean I don't have peer pressure today? No. I have made sure to surround myself with the kind of peer pressure that can help me. My friends in the Lord inspire me and hold me accountable to do the right thing and be a man of God. These friends would never let me brag about looking at pornography, talk badly about Karen, or cheat on her without confronting me about it. And I would hold them to the same accountability. That's the right kind of peer pressure. No friend is perfect, but we need to have friends who share our values and confront us when we violate them.

DEPENDENCY #5: WISE COUNSELORS

Joab, one of David's commanders, was a constant source of wise counsel. David had others under his leadership who were there simply to give him wise counsel. In fact, it seemed that anytime David heard of a man who was particularly wise, he would call for that man and listen to him. Notice that the single time David ignored Joab, about conducting the census, the results were catastrophic.

We need to surround ourselves with wise counsel. One area in which this is seen every day is in business. I have seen people fail in business, though not because they did not have a good business model or business sense. Instead, they failed simply because they would not listen to outside counsel. They would not call in consultants when they needed them, even though the fact is, we all need the counsel of those with experience and success in their lives. We need wisdom from experts in finance, medicine, education, relationships, and other fields.

Proverbs repeats the vital necessity of this dependency many times:

> Where *there is* no counsel, the people fall;
> But in the multitude of counselors *there is* safety
> (Proverbs 11:14).

> Without counsel, plans go awry,
> But in the multitude of counselors they are established
> (Proverbs 15:22).

> By wise counsel you will wage your own war,
> And in a multitude of counselors *there is* safety
> (Proverbs 24:6).

These proverbs were not written by someone who knew nothing. They were given by Solomon, the wisest man in the history of the world apart from Jesus Christ. More than a dozen times in Proverbs, Solomon speaks of the need for good counsel.

OPPOSITION TO HONEST DEPENDENCE

Two major barriers keep us from taking these five steps into dependence. In some ways, they are two sides of the same coin.

OBSTACLE #1: PRIDE

First, we must overcome pride. Pride does not want to admit weaknesses. A worldly, humanistic confidence in our own ability won't admit to weaknesses. That prideful attitude is ingrained in the world's way of thinking.

Pride was part of King Saul's life, and it was the reason God rejected him. The apostle Paul, on the other hand, did not allow pride to rule in his life nor cause him to hide his areas of weakness:

> Lest I should be exalted above measure by the abundance of the revelations, a thorn in the flesh was given to me, a messenger of Satan to buffet me, lest I be exalted above measure. Concerning this thing I pleaded with the Lord three times that it might depart from me. And He said to me, "My grace is sufficient for you, for My strength is made perfect in weakness." Therefore most gladly I will rather boast in my infirmities, that the power of Christ may rest upon me. Therefore I take pleasure in infirmities, in reproaches, in needs, in persecutions, in distresses, for Christ's sake. For when I am weak, then I am strong (2 Corinthians 12:7–10).

The truth is, God is neither ashamed nor limited by our weaknesses if we will acknowledge them and turn to His provision. When Paul cried out for God to take away a thorn in his flesh, the Lord responded, "Paul, My grace is

194

sufficient for you. For My power is made perfect in your weakness."

 God is neither ashamed nor limited by our weaknesses if we will acknowledge them and turn to His provision.

Many of us feel like God wants to reject us because we are weak. We are convinced He will not work through us because we don't know enough, aren't gifted enough, and we have hang-ups and problems. We think God is in heaven saying, "Listen, when you finally get it together, I'll do something with you. But in the meantime, you are such a mess that I don't even want talk to you about you serving Me."

But God's perspective is totally different: "Hey, do you think all your problems were hidden from Me when I called you? Do you think that limits Me? Let Me tell you something: your weaknesses are actually My opportunities. Give your weakness to Me, for My grace is sufficient for you."

Grace means unmerited favor. It means God chose you for no *earthly* reason. It means you don't deserve it. All you have to do is come to your Daddy and ask, and He will give it to you. Pride blinds us from discovering the freedom and provision God offers us because it keeps us from admitting we are weak.

OBSTACLE #2: INSECURITY

A second barrier to godly dependence is insecurity. Insecurity is feeling as though we are defective and there is something wrong with us because we're incomplete and imperfect. This does not mean insecure people always act insecurely. The truth is, many hide their insecurities behind an area of strength, which is why it is difficult to separate from pride. This is what Samson did. Despite Samson's size and strength, he failed to follow God in every other area. He was a weak and immoral man. One night, after sleeping with a prostitute, he went to the gates of the city, tore them off their hinges, carried them to the top of the hill, and dropped them. Why? He was trying to use his strength as a covering for his immorality.

There are many ways people can make a show of strength to hide their insecurities. They may use money as a cover for how weak they are. Or they may constantly bring attention to their looks, their athletic abilities, or their personalities, hoping people will not see the insecurity that has them crippled. They hope no one else will see the things they believe make them defective.

Other people deal with insecurities in a different way. They talk openly and frequently about their deficiencies. But they are not doing it to be transparent or to seek help. Instead, they are holding it up as the ultimate failure and an excuse to avoid moving ahead: "Well, I just can't take on that challenge or opportunity because of this failure in my life." That is another manifestation of insecurity.

I spent most of my life as an insecure person. Today, without God, I would still be extremely insecure. There is no way I can do what God has called me to do without Him and good people around me. Until I discovered that, I was held captive to insecurity. I knew what God wanted to do with my life, but instead of trusting in Him to accomplish it, I measured myself and felt totally inadequate and insecure. I hid behind a facade of confidence, standing with my chest out as if ready to conquer the world. All the time, inside I was a shivering little boy, terrified of waking up every morning. That's what insecurity does.

Security says, "Yes, I'm afraid and weak. And I am also gifted. In those areas in which I am weak, I thank God that there is someone else who knows what to do. In those areas in which I am strong, I remind myself that my strength is incomplete in itself. I need God, and I need to be surrounded by the strengths of others who can complement and complete me."

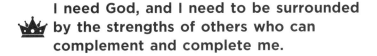

> **I need God, and I need to be surrounded by the strengths of others who can complement and complete me.**

You can choose to sit and grovel over your weakness, you can deny it and pretend it doesn't exist, or you can declare, "Yes, I am a weak person, but I have a powerful God. He is my strength. He is my shield. And He is my refuge. Furthermore, I am a connected person. I am surrounded by people who give me strength where I'm weak. They supply the armor and weapons in my life that are missing. I understand my limitations, and I have surrounded myself with good people I can depend on—people who make me whole. Because I'm connected and accountable, I am safe and can continue to go where God wants me to go."

You have a call on your life, and God wants you to get there. And you *can* get there. David's life is a good example of how you overcome some of the obstacles that block your way.

Part Seven

THE WHISPERER OF PRIDE

DEPEND ON GOD AND GIVE HIM THE GLORY

HERE IS THE eighth truth about greatness: great men and women are those who humbly depend upon God and give Him the praise and glory He deserves.

At this point in David's life, he had turned from his sins against Uriah and Bathsheba. He had shown wisdom in choosing to walk in humility, transparency, accountability, and counsel. It might appear that he had closed every door to the enemy's access while successfully stepping into his destiny.

A WHISPER THAT DEFEATS WARRIORS

Sadly, there is one tactic Satan will try to use on every great man or woman of God. That is exactly what he did to King David at the height of his greatest witness to the wisdom and power of God in his life. And though not nearly as imposing as Goliath's spear, that simple tactic proved most effective in prompting David to make a tragic decision at the peak of his reign.

We read the account in 1 Chronicles 21:

> Now Satan stood up against Israel, and moved David to number Israel. So David said to Joab and to the leaders

of the people, "Go, number Israel from Beersheba to Dan, and bring the number of them to me that I may know *it*."

And Joab answered, "May the Lord make His people a hundred times more than they are. But, my lord the king, *are* they not all my lord's servants? Why then does my lord require this thing? Why should he be a cause of guilt in Israel?"

Nevertheless the king's word prevailed against Joab. Therefore Joab departed and went throughout all Israel and came to Jerusalem. Then Joab gave the sum of the number of the people to David. All Israel *had* one million one hundred thousand men who drew the sword, and Judah *had* four hundred and seventy thousand men who drew the sword. But he did not count Levi and Benjamin among them, for the king's word was abominable to Joab.

And God was displeased with this thing; therefore He struck Israel. So David said to God, "I have sinned greatly, because I have done this thing; but now, I pray, take away the iniquity of Your servant, for I have done very foolishly." And the Lord spoke to Gad, David's seer, saying, "Go and tell David, saying, 'Thus says the Lord: "I offer you three things; choose one of them for yourself, that I may do it to you."'"

So Gad came to David and said to him, "Thus says the Lord: 'Choose for yourself, either three years of famine, or three months to be defeated by your foes with the sword of your enemies overtaking *you*, or else for three days the sword of the Lord—the plague in the land, with the angel of the Lord destroying throughout all the territory of Israel.' Now consider what answer I should take back to Him who sent me."

And David said to Gad, "I am in great distress. Please let me fall into the hand of the Lord, for His mercies *are* very great; but do not let me fall into the hand of man."

So the Lord sent a plague upon Israel, and seventy thousand men of Israel fell. And God sent an angel to Jerusalem to destroy it. As he was destroying, the Lord looked and relented of the disaster, and said to the angel who was destroying, "It is enough; now restrain your hand" (vv. 1–15).

This incident took place toward the end of David's reign. He had been extremely successful, defeating one enemy after the other and attaining great riches and power. But he took what God had given him and began to take personal credit for it. David decided he would measure his strength by a standard other than the favor of God.

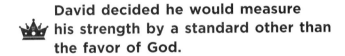 **David decided he would measure his strength by a standard other than the favor of God.**

How did Satan do what the spear of a giant and the swords of armies had not been able to do? How did he get a man of such success and stature before God to make such a tragic mistake?

He did it with a whisper—*the whisper of pride.*

FROM BLESSED TO ARROGANT

What was so unwise about King David's decision? Why was taking a numerical census of the people such a huge sin in the eyes of God? After all, every ten years we take a census in the United States. Not only that, but doesn't history record numerous stories of leaders and kings who were naturally arrogant? What was the difference between them and King David?

203

The difference was that David was chosen as king by God Himself. The people did not choose him. The king of Israel was not the representative of the people; he was the representative of God Himself. When David took the census, he strayed from his loyalty to God.

David's sin was in his motive. He was counting the people—specifically arms-bearing men—as a way to measure and demonstrate his accomplishments and strength as king. He lost sight of the fact that his strength had always come from God alone, not through any personal ability or military might. It didn't matter how many capable soldiers Israel had in its army, because the trust of the nation had been in God. David had won many battles in the past—including with Goliath—without the help of any military men.

David's captain, Joab, was keenly aware of this fact. He knew that by taking a census, his king wanted to establish how great he had become. So Joab challenged David's decision: "Why are you making us go and count all the people? Do you not know that every person in Israel is the servant of the Lord? They are all the Lord's servants." In his arrogance, David disregarded Joab's warning. This was an instance where David did not heed wise counsel. The irony was this: the numbering of the people of Israel could not measure David's greatness. It could only establish how much God had blessed him.

The question every great person of God must ask is, *How much can God bless me before I use it against Him?* A naturally attractive person may look in a mirror and become arrogant about his or her appearance. A person blessed with the ability to accumulate wealth has an opportunity to become arrogant, independent, and unteachable. In thousands of different ways, men and women who have been richly blessed by God may credit themselves for that blessing and forget the true Source of all they have. That was David's sin.

As an untrained shepherd boy armed with only with a slingshot, David had trusted God to help him defeat a man who was a giant in strength, stature, and military experience. God alone gave David victory over all Israel's enemies, promoted him, and made him great.

One day, however, David decided to praise himself instead of God. That day he may have woken up declaring, "You know, I am powerful. I am handsome. I have the most beautiful women in Israel as my wives and concubines. All my enemies fear me. I have killed giants. You must admit it—I am great. What can I do to measure just how great I have become?" David took what God had given him and attributed the glory to himself. That day was the beginning of a bitter time for a blessed nation.

WHAT WENT WRONG?

This incident in David's life raises an important question for you and me. If a man marked by his humility and adoration of the Lord could slip so quickly into an act of arrogance, how can we recognize and close the door to such temptation and devastation in our own lives before it is too late?

Actually, it's not hard at all when we understand how Satan gained his opportunity. The answer is revealed in the first words of 1 Chronicles 21: "Now Satan stood up against Israel, and moved David to number Israel" (v. 1). Satan stood up against Israel, and he stands up against us all the time. To see how he does that, look at this same story as it is told in 2 Samuel 24:1: "Again the anger of the Lord was aroused against Israel and He [God] moved David against them to say, 'Go, number Israel and Judah.'"

One account says Satan did it. The other says God prompted David. So was it God, or was it Satan? There is a big difference between the two, you know. But this is no contradiction. It was both!

When Satan is allowed to stand up against us, we have a bigger problem than just the devil. Satan can come against us only when we step out from under God's covering of protection. In David's life, at that point, God saw the pride in David's heart and actions, so He lifted His protection. David's actions gave Satan the opportunity he needed. In both accounts, Satan was clearly the agent that stood up against David and incited him to commit a sin. God does not incite us to commit a sin, but He will lift His protection when we become arrogant.

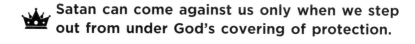 **Satan can come against us only when we step out from under God's covering of protection.**

GOD HATES PRIDE, NOT PEOPLE

Two powerful scriptural principles are at work here.

First, God does not hate people, even prideful people. However, He does *hate* pride. Proverbs 6:16–17 says,

> These six *things* the Lord hates,
> Yes, seven are an abomination to Him:
> A proud look ...

Notice, first on the list of seven things God hates is "a proud look."

Not only does God hate pride, but He also actively *resists* it. James 4:6 says, "God resists the proud, but gives grace to the humble." That God resists the proud should be no surprise, but what might shock us is how strong that resistance is. This word "resist" does not depict one person standing his ground, trying to stop another from making progress. Rather it describes an entire military battalion set up to ensure that the opposing force has no chance of succeeding.

So when we read "God resists the proud," we can be sure that God has vowed that pride will never succeed. He hates it and is committed to fighting against it with overwhelming force. He is saying, "If you keep going the way of pride, I Myself will fight you. Keep walking in arrogance, and you will find yourself up against everything I am. I am going to set Myself in battle formation against you."

Look again at the last half of James 4:6: "But [God] gives grace to the humble." Just as God is fierce in His resistance to pride, so also to an even greater degree He pours out blessings on the humble. That God "gives grace" means He gives every blessing you can imagine. God's grace is so much more than giving us a break or a making us a way out of a difficult situation. When God gives grace to the humble, He releases tremendous blessing because He loves humility:

> Submit to God. Resist the devil and he will flee from you. Draw near to God and He will draw near to you. Cleanse *your* hands, *you* sinners; and purify *your* hearts, *you* double-minded. Lament and mourn and weep! Let your laughter be turned to mourning and *your* joy to gloom. Humble yourselves in the sight of the Lord, and He will lift you up (James 4:7–10).

God hates the little smirk that comes when we begin to think we have done anything without Him. That look that can come when a tight financial situation turns around and we are tempted to think, *I have a lot of money. I can handle anything that comes along.* Or that look that attributes our giftings and talents to our own efforts: *Look how gifted I am! Look how strong I am! Look how talented I am!*

Indicators that we are beginning to think we can do it without God are clear. Lack of prayer is the most obvious—anything we do not pray about is something we think we can do without God. Prayerlessness is godlessness. Anything we are not praying about in our lives—our money, our jobs, our relationships—is something we think we can handle without God. And an area we think we can succeed in without God's help is an area of separation from Him and from His provision in our lives.

Now we can understand why God has vowed that He will never allow pride to succeed in our lives. He will never let pride go unopposed. He lifts His hand of blessing and protection, not passively, but in active opposition to pride. He says, "Hey, if you want to do this on your own, get ready for some resistance—not because I do not love you, but because I do love you. I hate the sin of pride that will destroy you. So don't think I am going to enable this behavior. I am not going to wink at it. Pride is a terrible, deadly sin, and I am going to fight both for you and against you because I love you too much to watch you self-destruct."

When you understand that truth, you will begin to see that so often the resistance you experience is not from the devil but from God. The resistance you are up against now, or may find yourself facing in the future, may be God resisting the pride that is causing you to try to do something without Him. Remember, every time God resists you, He is resisting you as a loving parent trying to keep you from going a self-destructive way. He does not hate you. Far from it! You are the apple of God's eye. He actively opposes pride because it is how Satan gains entrance into your life. It is, as 1 Chronicles 21:1 describes it, Satan's opportunity to stand up against us—to stand up just as the lion does in the instant before it pounces on its prey.

THE PROWLING LION

Karen and I have had the opportunity to go to Africa, where we watched lions hunting in the bush. If you have ever been on a safari or watched a documentary about lions, you can imagine what a fascinating adventure that was for us. What we learned while observing the natural habits of lions was significant for our spiritual understanding. It was an object lesson showing us how the devil tries to interrupt and bring down believers who have attained success on the path to greatness in God. The apostle Peter points to this parallel in 1 Peter 5:8: "Your adversary the devil walks about like a roaring lion, seeking whom he may devour."

If you know how lions feed, you may remember that it is the female lions that do the hunting. Crouching low with their heads right against the ground, they begin to watch and stalk their prey. Their bodies stay hidden below the grass line, with their eyes above it just enough to observe their targets. When an animal becomes separated from the herd, lions will seize that opportunity to stand up on their hindquarters and pounce on their prey.

This image will help us understand the first words of the tragic account of King David taking a census. When the Bible records that "Satan stood up" (1 Chronicles 21:1), it means Satan had been looking for an opportunity to get into David's life, and he finally found it and then pounced upon it. Though the enemy's attempts had been frustrated many times before, he kept prowling and watching and waiting for just the right opportunity to take David down. Satan's chance came when

David decided to take a census that displayed pride in the strength of his army. That prideful act caused God to step back and lift His protection. David's sin gave Satan just the opportunity he had been looking for, and the enemy stood up to strike.

If you are questioning whether Satan really is able to do this to us, let me assure you: he absolutely can and will. Without exception, every single time we begin walking in sin, especially the sin of pride, Satan will stand up and come against us. That was the warning Peter emphasized when he talked about how vital it is to walk free of pride:

> You younger people, submit yourselves to *your* elders. Yes, all of *you* be submissive to one another, and be clothed with humility, for
> "God resists the proud,
> But gives grace to the humble."
> Therefore humble yourselves under the mighty hand of God, that He may exalt you in due time, casting all your care upon Him, for He cares for you.
> Be sober, be vigilant; because your adversary the devil walks about like a roaring lion, seeking whom he may devour. Resist him, steadfast in the faith, knowing that the same sufferings are experienced by your brotherhood in the world (1 Peter 5:5–9).

Because of what we know of the lion's hunting tactics, we can understand the kind of threat the devil poses and how vulnerable we become to his attack when pride takes root in our lives. We must choose to clothe ourselves with humility, be willing to submit to our elders, and be humble toward each other. That is the only way to protect ourselves against an enemy crouched and ready to stand up and pounce on us the instant he is given an opportunity. We must not be deceived about this in the least. Satan has no trouble at all recognizing the sin of pride. Remember, after all, that pride was his original sin.

DOUBLE CURSE OR DOUBLE BLESSING?

With pride at the core of our enemy's true nature, no wonder he is so diligent in his attempts to use that sin against us. Pride is a double-edged sword carrying a double curse. First, it causes God to withdraw from us and to oppose us at the same time. We walk out from under God's protection simply by declaring that we do not need God. God will not violate our decision, nor will He cooperate with that deception by enabling our prideful independence. In removing Himself from any agreement with pride, He honors our declaration of independence from Him. When we are out from under God's protection, we open the door to a second curse—we give the devil an opportunity to do whatever he wants to do.

There is something far more powerful than the double curse of pride, however, and that is the double blessing of humility. When we surrender to God and submit to Him, we are choosing to walk in humility. And as we do so, God gives us the ability to resist Satan and all his strategies. The double blessing of humility is that God protects and blesses us, and the devil cannot have us. That is what we want in every area of our lives—for our children and every relationship, in our finances, in our health, and so on. He may be crouched and prowling nearby as he looks for an opening, but if we continue to walk in submission to authority, honor people, be humble, and submit ourselves to God, the devil cannot pounce on our families, our finances, or our influence. Humility insulates us from Satan's attack.

The double blessing of humility is that God protects and blesses us, and the devil cannot have us.

By rejecting pride, we reject the double curse and choose to walk in the double blessing of protection and provision.

WILL YOU TURN THE BLESSING AGAINST GOD?

I think all of us would say that we would choose a double blessing instead of a double curse. If the devil approached us and gave us that choice, we'd have no problem choosing blessing. If he approached us with an obvious roar, we would be quick to run from his attack.

Think about how you would respond if the devil knocked on your door, and when you opened it, he announced, "I am the devil. I am cursed from eternity past to eternity future. My goal is to steal from, kill, and destroy as many people as possible. In fulfilling that mission, I often use pride to open the door into people's lives. Interested in joining the team?"

You know what you would say: "Get out of here, devil. There is no way I am going to become part of your gang or agenda!"

But just as the lion does not roar until after the opportunity to take its prey, so our enemy approaches in silence. He may stalk us as a roaring lion, but he approaches us like he approached King David—*with the whisper of pride*. The devil never obviously presents himself as the devil. He is subtle and wrapped in a disguise. Rather than come as the prince of darkness, he presents himself as an angel of light.

Before the roar of destruction is the *whisper* of pride—words that appeal to our flesh and seductively seek our agreement:

Boy, you are good looking.
Girl, you are so talented!
Aren't you something! Look at your place in society.
You are special. You are smarter and more talented than anyone else.
You have so much more wisdom than anyone around you. You are not like others who need to be submitted. You are strong. You can handle things on your own.
I'm telling you—you are something else!

Because these thoughts come as a whisper, we do not readily recognize them as being from the devil. In fact, sometimes the whisper of pride does not originate with the devil—it comes from our own thoughts. That makes it no less dangerous. When we entertain prideful thoughts and agree with them, regardless of the process, we become arrogant. As we become puffed up, the devil seizes that opportunity and pounces before we even know what's happened.

TAKING CREDIT FOR GOD'S BLESSINGS

There should be no real surprises in what I'm telling you. After all, according to the Bible, Satan was the first being to ever commit the sin of pride. Before his fall, the devil was incredibly beautiful and talented. He was the archangel who was the worship leader in all of heaven. The Lord addressed Satan through the prophet Ezekiel when the devil manifested in the king of Tyre:

> You *were* the seal of perfection,
> Full of wisdom and perfect in beauty.
> You were in Eden, the garden of God;
> Every precious stone *was* your covering:
> The sardius, topaz, and diamond,

Beryl, onyx, and jasper,
Sapphire, turquoise, and emerald with gold.
The workmanship of your timbrels and pipes
Was prepared for you on the day you were created.
You *were* the anointed cherub who covers;
I established you;
You were on the holy mountain of God;
You walked back and forth in the midst of fiery stones.
You *were* perfect in your ways from the day you were created,
Till iniquity was found in you.
By the abundance of your trading
You became filled with violence within,
And you sinned;
Therefore I cast you as a profane thing
Out of the mountain of God;
And I destroyed you, O covering cherub,
From the midst of the fiery stones.
Your heart was lifted up because of your beauty;
You corrupted your wisdom for the sake of your splendor;
I cast you to the ground,
I laid you before kings,
That they might gaze at you (Ezekiel 28:12–17).

In these verses, we can see that the first sin in the universe was committed by an angel with a free will. God created this favored angel with wisdom and beauty, with musical instruments built into his body. He was a covering cherub assigned a position of ministry in the very presence of God. Then one day, as he was worshipping God and giving God the glory He deserved, he looked away from God and stared at himself and said something like, "Whoa, you are really something!"

Isaiah 14 records the devil's words as "I am going to be like God. I am going to have a throne. I am going to set my throne on the mountain" (see verses 13–14). *I ... I ... I.*

Satan corrupted himself, the Bible says, because he focused on his own beauty. But who gave him that beauty? Who established him? Is it not interesting that the very thing Satan used against God was the gift and ability God had given him? That same temptation is the one with which Satan approaches us today.

When Satan committed sin, a third of the angels followed him in rebellion. That tells us how incredibly persuasive and powerful he had been in heaven. Think about the fact that even though he and his troops were still outnumbered two to one by the good angels (not to mention that they were going up against God Almighty), Satan was able to convince such a sizable number of angels to follow him in his rebellion.

And when God hovered over the formless void of this earth and recreated it, the devil was present here with his demons (the angels who had followed him). In the Garden of Eden, this once most beautiful of all beings, now corrupted by what he did with that beauty, seized the opportunity to whisper pride into the ears of the crown jewels of God's creation—Adam and Eve. Laying aside their own glory, this blessed couple listened to and followed the enemy. Their son Cain heard that same whisper and went on to kill his brother, Abel. Satan tickled King David's ear with pride. And so it went down through the ages until even now.

Satan has continued to use the same tactic at every opportunity. He's caused untold millions of good, godly people to fall in this way. Given an open door, he will whisper in our ears and cause us to think we are special—not because of the One who has made us everything we are but because of our own ability. That's the way Satan fell, so he knows it will work. And he never stops whispering in our ears, hoping that one day we will begin thinking we have gained what we have by our own efforts. He's hoping we'll begin to think, *I do not*

215

have to submit to anybody. After all, I've got it. I am somebody. I excel at everything I do without needing any help. I don't need to pray.

Satan's fall as a result of pride raises that crucial question we all must ask ourselves: how much can God give us before we use it against him?

THE DILEMMA OF A LOVING GOD

This potential for people to be tempted to take personal credit for what God has done for them creates a dilemma. God loves human beings above all the rest of creation. His desire is to pour out blessings beyond measure and help His children succeed in achieving their full potential in Him.

A good, loving, giving Creator would never create a bunch of robot pawns incapable of making a choice. God has called His people to be the bride of Christ. We are designed to rule and reign with Him throughout all of eternity. When God created mankind, He created us in His own image. He created us with the ability to make choices. We get to determine how we will live our lives, whom we will serve, and where we will spend eternity.

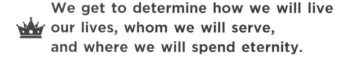

We get to determine how we will live our lives, whom we will serve, and where we will spend eternity.

Our Creator is not an insecure, neurotic God bent on trying to hold us down through manipulation and control. We need to settle this fact in our minds. Every act of our Creator is designed to lift us up to the highest levels and give us the whole kingdom of God. Remember what Jesus Himself said about our Father's purposes for us:

> Do not fear, little flock, for it is your Father's good pleasure to give you the kingdom (Luke 12:32).

> Seek first the kingdom of God and His righteousness, and all these things shall be added to you (Matthew 6:33)

These verses are a direct contradiction of Satan's lie that God is trying to keep something from us. Jesus said that if we will set our focus and purpose on first seeking the kingdom of God and His righteousness, we will discover that it is our Father's desire to give it all to us. He is trying to share everything He has with us.

God has withheld nothing good from us. Yet so many people have taken His gifts and turned against Him. They have abandoned the glorious riches of a kingdom in which they were destined to rule and reign for the temporary trinkets of a deposed and defeated enemy who whispered in their ear that what they have and who they are is a result of their own power.

STAYING HUNGRY AND HUMBLE

In the first home prayer group we started several years ago, there was a precious couple who had started a business. They were two of the humblest people I had ever met. Every week, they were the first people on our doorstep. No one was more faithful to those midweek meetings. They were so teachable, always saying things like "Jimmy, what about this? Karen, what about that?" They were hungry for God and His Word.

During that time, their business became increasingly successful, which was a wonderful thing, but gradually the husband began to have a change of heart. In little more than two years, his attitude went from one of total humility to one of total arrogance. One of the most hungry, teachable people I had ever met became equally as arrogant, unteachable, and ungodly.

One day, I took him out to lunch so I could tell him how much I cared about him and to share my concerns about the turn his life had taken. He did not like it. Immediately they stopped coming to our life group and quit coming to church. At that point, this couple answered the question about how much God could give them before they turned it against Him.

The next report I received was that they were having significant marriage problems. Then I lost contact with them, never knowing if they got things turned around in their lives; never knowing if they turned back toward God.

What that precious couple encountered is no different than what will happen to any one of us if we start listening to and believing the whisper of pride. Just as they did, each of us will have an opportunity to determine how much God can give us before we use it against Him.

Of course, we do not have to turn against God because of those things He has uniquely gifted us with and those blessings He brings into our possession. If we will choose to reject the whisper of pride, remember who our true Source is, and be grateful for all we are and have in Him, we will inherit the kingdom.

Two of the most significant people in my life happen to be a couple of considerable wealth. One of the most interesting things I have noticed about them is that the more they prosper, the humbler they become. They are not letting riches and blessings drive them from God. The more resources He gives them, the more resources they use for Him and His purposes. It does not have to end in disaster.

THE CHOICE IS OURS

We do have a choice. How much God can give you or me without us using it against Him is a choice each of us has to make. I have to make that choice in the ministry God has given Karen and me. It is my choice to say, "God, no matter how much You bless me, I will never lose my hunger for and dependence on You. I will use what You give me to advance the kingdom of Your love. I have made the decision that I will not become arrogant by delighting in the whisper that I am the be-all and the end-all of the anointing." It is not enough for me to simply make that choice. I must also work at it. I know my own disposition toward arrogance. Being humble is not my natural tendency. My natural tendency is to be self-reliant and prideful.

That prideful way of thinking was birthed in our original sin nature. We are born with a bent toward pride and arrogance. It's in our nature to take credit for those things that only should be credited to God. That's why I must purpose to work at this thing for the rest of my life. In order for my Father's dream to be fulfilled in me, I have chosen to walk gratefully before God. The more blessings He pours out on us, the humbler we must become. And the humbler we become, the more we use those resources for Him, all the while thanking Him for the power to stay faithful to that decision. Despite our humanity, God will back us up in that decision. Because He does, I can say that everything God has given to Karen and me, we have used for Him. And I purpose to be able to say the same thing one year from now and ten years from now.

I never want to have to say, "God, withhold from me so I will not be tempted and fall into pride." No, I choose to say, "God, I want to walk, to live, to speak, and to act in such a way that You can freely give me more and more. Give me prosperity so I can be a blessing to those You love and care for those who are lost and hurting. I desire and purpose to give glory to Your name throughout the earth."

I believe that prayer is the heart cry of every believer who learns to recognize and resist the whisper of pride. It was David's heart cry until that day he agreed with Satan's whisper and opened a dark chapter in his life. But the good news for him (and for you and me) is that God forgives. Israel's king repented, and at his death David was remembered as an honorable man in good standing with God. We all have had times of darkness in our lives. They may not have been as costly as David's, but still the prideful choices we've made have cost us dearly.

Just remember this: God loves you more than you can ever understand. And He desires to give to you more each day than you can imagine. What He has in store for you is increasingly above all you could ask or think—a life overflowing in abundance of success in relationships, emotional and physical health, finances, and every other area of life. He desires to pour out His blessings on you until your cup runs over and spills onto others and you fulfill your destiny in every detail.

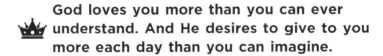

God loves you more than you can ever understand. And He desires to give to you more each day than you can imagine.

Only you set the limit of how much God can give you before you use it against Him. The windows of heaven are ready to be opened over every believer. But for those blessings to be poured out, we must be humble people. We must take time alone with our Father and examine our motives and lives. We must ask Him to search our hearts and show us the things we need to correct. We must ask Him to help us recognize and resist the whisper of pride.

THE FORMULA FOR GLORY

Twice in the book of Isaiah, God says He will not give His glory to another (Isaiah 42:8; 48:11). This truth is revealed throughout the Scriptures and graphically demonstrated in David's sin of pride. David became a truly great person and a man after God's own heart when his focus was on the Lord.

However, when David began to focus on how great he had become and decided to take the census, he robbed God of His glory and took glory for himself. There is a simple formula in the Bible: *To the degree we take God's glory is to the same degree He takes ours.*

Remember that formula and notice in the Bible and in life how it works every single time. There is another side to the formula, however, that is much more encouraging. It is this: *When we give God the glory He deserves, He shares His glory with us.* God will not give His glory to another, but He will share it with those who live to glorify Him.

This was true of David beginning at the battle line against Goliath. Because David gave God glory, the Lord also glorified David and continued to do so for many years, even to the present day. The greatest revelation of this truth was seen in the life of Jesus, a descendant of David. He lived His life to give glory to His Father and declined taking glory for Himself. The result was that God highly exalted Jesus

221

and bestowed upon Him a Name above every other name (Philippians 2:9–11). Humbly depend on God and give Him the glory He deserves, and He will give you glory.

A Prayer for Humility

Heavenly Father,

Right now, as truthfully and humbly as I know to approach You, I turn away from the sin of pride and independence. I repent for allowing myself to believe things about myself that are not true. The truth is, You made me in my mother's womb. And without exception, every single gift—every point of intellect, every ability, every talent, every ability to acquire wealth, everything that is good—You gave me.

If I find favor with others, that favor comes from You, Lord. Every promotion I have received, or ever will receive, comes from You. Every position I am given, it is You, Lord, who's given it to me. You exalt, and You tear down. Everything comes from You.

I willingly change my heart and mind and repent of ever attributing anything to myself and robbing You of the glory in those things that only come from You. I repent, God, of making decisions without consulting You, as though I were able to navigate my own life without Your wisdom and counsel. I repent of vain imaginations and of dwelling on self-promoting thoughts.

I regret that I have ever given the devil any opportunity to stand up, enter in, and devour—to steal, kill, and destroy—in any area of my life. You never intended for that to happen. You never gave my enemy that much power. I did it. Just as I opened that door, so I now slam shut that door to the enemy's intrusion as I humble myself before You and exalt You alone as Lord of my life.

I repent of the pride that gave an opening to the enemy who stalks me, looking for opportunity to rise up against me and pounce on me. I submit to You, Father, and in You I resist the devil and command him to leave. I command him, by Your Word and in the power of the name of Jesus, to flee from my family, my marriage, my health, and every other area of my life.

As I humble myself before You, Lord, I thank You for protecting and blessing me. Right now I want to answer the question of how much You can give me without me using it against You. I declare that You can give me everything You want to give me, and I will always use it to honor and serve You.

That is my heart's desire. That is my commitment before You and in the strength You provide.

I give You the glory that You and You alone deserve. In Jesus' mighty name, Amen.

Part Eight

THE SELF-ENCOURAGER

OVERCOME DISCOURAGEMENT AND ACHIEVE YOUR DESTINY

IF PRIDE APPROACHES the believer with a whisper, then another of the enemy's weapons arrives with a shout. That is the weapon of discouragement.

David was particularly effective against this common ploy of the devil. And nowhere is this clearer than in a desperate situation recorded in 1 Samuel 30:1–8:

> Now it happened, when David and his men came to Ziklag, on the third day, that the Amalekites had invaded the South and Ziklag, attacked Ziklag and burned it with fire, and had taken captive the women and those who *were* there, from small to great; they did not kill anyone, but carried *them* away and went their way. So David and his men came to the city, and there it was, burned with fire; and their wives, their sons, and their daughters had been taken captive.
>
> Then David and the people who *were* with him lifted up their voices and wept, until they had no more power to weep. And David's two wives, Ahinoam the Jezreelitess, and Abigail the widow of Nabal the Carmelite, had been taken captive. Now David was greatly distressed, for the people spoke of stoning him, because the soul of all the people was grieved, every man for his sons and his

daughters. But David strengthened himself in the Lord his God.

Then David said to Abiathar the priest, Ahimelech's son, "Please bring the ephod here to me." And Abiathar brought the ephod to David. So David inquired of the Lord, saying, "Shall I pursue this troop? Shall I overtake them?" And He answered him, "Pursue, for you shall surely overtake *them* and without fail recover *all*."

It is impossible to overstate the deep emotion of this devastating event. In retrospect, we know this story has a happy ending, because David becomes king of Israel. But at Ziklag, David could have easily fallen into despair and given up on God's promise. What is so important for us to see is the way David pulled himself out of what must have been one of the lowest points of his life.

Although there was no outward evidence to support it at the time, David was on the threshold of his destiny to fulfill the promise and calling of God for his life. The devil came against David with everything he could muster. And the devil does battle against believers in the same way today.

One of the most exciting experiences of your life as a child of God is coming alive to your greatness in God. At the same time, it is one of the most devastating things that can happen to the kingdom of darkness. For that reason, the devil will do all he can to discourage you. He will work his hardest to stop God's dream for your life from happening.

One reason this old demonic tool of discouragement remains effective is because it is so easy to deploy. Satan can take any situation in your life and use it to try to discourage you. Challenges with your health, finances, family, and job are just some of the areas he can tap into to raise up discouragement as a weapon against you.

Considering how dependent the devil is on this tactic, he must have found David particularly frustrating. David handled setbacks remarkably well. As you focus on being a great man or woman of God, give special attention to the way David stood against despair and defeat at Ziklag.

Consider again what the Bible says Israel's future king did at one of the lowest points in his life. Most people would have folded under the pressure, but not David. Instead, he strengthened and encouraged himself in the Lord. This is the ninth truth about greatness: every great man or woman of God must overcome times of darkness and deep discouragement in order to achieve his or her destiny in God.

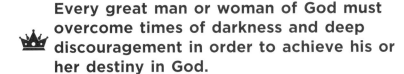 **Every great man or woman of God must overcome times of darkness and deep discouragement in order to achieve his or her destiny in God.**

The devil will use discouragement at key times in your life to try to overwhelm and defeat you. But you can overcome him as you learn to encourage yourself in the Lord.

A FUTURE KING IN FLIGHT

To get the full impact of this story, step back a few years into David's life. David really showed up on the scene when Samuel the prophet appeared at his house and anointed David as king. Samuel carried out this anointing in secret. Saul, the reigning king at the time, knew nothing about it. David's father, Jesse, was even caught off guard by Samuel's act. The youngest of his eight sons was Jesse's last pick for the future king of the nation—but David was God's first pick. As significant as it was for the future of Israel, David's anointing was an unpublicized, private event.

However, David received quite a bit of publicity related to another event. The people broadcast his name throughout Israel when he killed Goliath. At first, it might seem that victory in battle would have made some sense for considering David as a potential heir to the throne. And although the king initially took the nation's celebrated champion into his house, Saul quickly shifted his favor to jealousy when he discovered this shepherd-warrior had gained more popularity than the king himself. David went from renowned victor to trying to protect his own life during Saul's fits of jealous rage. Before long, Saul was making deliberate attempts to kill David.

In 1 Samuel 20–26, David eventually fled from place to place throughout Israel from Saul's murderous pursuit. Even though God was obviously protecting David, he still faced real danger from Saul's plot. Then, in 1 Samuel 27, David feigned loyalty to Israel's most dangerous enemies, the Philistines. He and his band of followers, whom he had picked up along the way, lived under the protection of the Philistine city of Ziklag. This defection would have been seen as bordering treason, like an American who immigrated to Russia during the height of the Cold War.

On top of that, David joined in league with the Philistine army. For a time, he kept favor with one of the Philistine warlords by raiding the camps of Israel's enemies and falsely reporting that he and his men were also pillaging the Israelites. Over time, other Philistine lords became so uncomfortable and distrustful of this arrangement that they had David and his men removed from the military camp. At this point, David walked through some of the most discouraging days of his life.

A CRITICAL DECISION IN A DARK HOUR

With the Philistines kicking David out of the camp and King Saul still in pursuit, David and his small army returned to Ziklag, where they had their homes, property, wives, and children. But upon their return, they found their base camp had been attacked by the Amalekites. Their enemy had taken their wives and children as prisoners and burned their homes to the ground. It was a devastating discovery. David and his men were without a country. Their families had been taken captive. All seemed lost. While we often think of women as easy criers, the Bible says these men wept until no more tears remained. That's a remarkable description for a group of battle-hardened warriors. They lay down and cried until their bodies had been wrung dry with grief.

As if the day had not gone badly enough, when David's band of followers finished crying, they started talking—and the subject turned sharply. They wanted to stone David to death. This day had quickly descended from bad to worse. Everything God promised started to look like one sick joke. Receiving Samuel's anointing from God and slaying Goliath were high points for David, but since then, one bad thing had followed another. Thus far, the transpiring events seemed like a mockery against God's call on David's life. Then the greatest mockery of all would have been David dying under the stones of his own men in a Philistine city. David bore no resemblance to a man anyone would think God had chosen as king. Instead, he looked more like the biggest loser and worst leader in the world.

Imagine the emotional and social turmoil David must have experienced. If you were reading this story for the first time, would you be surprised to read David had fled for his life or, at the very least, threw up his hands and slipped silently back to the shepherd's field to spend the rest of his days in anonymity? Many of us would lose all confidence in ourselves and God at this point. Yet amazingly, David did none of those things. He didn't let himself give in to discouragement, nor did he sink into despair. He did not give up and quit. How did he keep from it?

Pay attention to what David did next. We have all been there before. We may not experience the same devastation that David did, but all of us have and will again experience some degree of what David went through that day. We know about the strong temptation to give in to despair at times like these.

But David *resisted*.

Given David's most recent experiences, all he could imagine was a life filled with running, while never really belonging anywhere in particular. Everything important had been stripped from him. And his future looked even worse—rejection and stoning at the hands of the men who had once believed in and followed him.

In that moment, David made his most crucial decision up to that point in his life. He "strengthened himself in the Lord his God" (1 Samuel 30:6). That word "strengthened" is also often translated "encouraged." That means David stopped in the middle of everything that was going on—the physical weariness, the emotional pain of personal loss, the thoughts that must have been screaming in his head, the rejection of those who had once trusted him—and he made a choice. David decided to *encourage* himself in God.

 **David decided to *encourage* himself in God.**

Satan was screaming in David's ear, "Look at what a loser you are! You have got to be the worst excuse for a leader in the history of the world! Obviously, God has changed His mind about anointing you as king." I believe the devil hurled every possible attack of condemnation and self-doubt at David while he was down. That is Satan's strategy for all of us.

Don't think David was any less human than you or I would be in that circumstance. We've been subject to demonic onslaughts. We've made mistakes and seen our enemy take every possible opportunity to turn them into accusations against us. He's waged a campaign to convince us that God cannot possibly use us anymore. We've battled thoughts that the One who created us for a great purpose and destiny in Him has now given up on us. Don't think the enemy was doing any less with David at that moment.

But David did not *take* those thoughts of discouragement. Instead, he *encouraged himself* in the Lord his God. When David made that decision, he heard a word from God—a word he shared with his men concerning God's plan to recover what was taken from them. It was actually a much bigger plan than they could have imagined.

The Amalekites raiders were a notorious bunch of robbers. So when God restored what was stolen from David and his men, He also gave them possession of all the goods the Amalekites had stolen from other towns and tribes throughout the region. Not only did David receive his family back, but he also became wealthy overnight! And it was all because he rejected despair over his circumstances and chose to encourage himself in the character and faithfulness of His God.

What David did not know was that at the same time this was taking place, God's hand of protection and favor had lifted from King Saul, and the king was killed in battle. David had every logical reason and opportunity to allow thoughts of discouragement and despair to overtake him. But those would not have been God's thoughts. The Lord's thoughts had not changed. Even in the darkest hour, God was still unfolding His plan for an unknown shepherd boy to become king and for an insignificant young nation to become known throughout the earth for its covenant with the living God.

Far from rejecting David, God had been steadily moving forward His plan for David to take his place as king, even during David's worst hour. There was no worldwide broadcast to show David the bigger picture of the events of that day. No cell phones or text messaging relayed the news of what was going on a country away. Without knowing how God was working things out, David chose to encourage himself in the One who had always been faithful to him. And by deciding not to slip into despair, he remained ready as he stepped into God's plan for him to sit on Israel's throne and lead that nation into greatness.

THE SECRETS OF SELF-ENCOURAGEMENT

God is always doing something beyond what we can see. That is what happened in David's life, and it is what is happening for us. Just as David had to choose to encourage himself in what God had said rather than give in to the visible circumstances and immediate emotions, so also you and I must follow David's example.

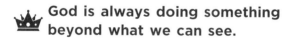 **God is always doing something beyond what we can see.**

The fact is, you *will* go through times of discouragement. Maybe you aren't facing major discouragement at the present, but it's inevitable in the future that you will face it. Discouragement and despair, if allowed to continue too long, will become dangerous and even deadly. The devil will work to convince you that you need to do the wrong thing or that God is finished with you. You may want to make a poor choice or give up entirely. Some people who face discouragement give up on their marriages, their families, and the call God has on their lives. They just simply give up.

But that does not have to be the case with you. Like David, you can choose to encourage and strengthen yourself in the Lord. I am going to take a deeper dive into the ways David always seemed able to encourage himself in the Lord. As I do, I pray you will discover that even in the worst of times, anyone can stay on the path to greatness in God by discovering and applying the four things that I call the secrets to self-encouragement.

SECRET #1: A TRUSTING RELATIONSHIP WITH GOD

The Decision to Trust

The first thing David did was to **make a conscious decision to trust God.** This is the first secret of self-encouragement. He was able to do this because he was always intently listening for God's voice. David followed a God who never discourages but always speaks to His people. Jesus said, "My sheep hear My voice" (John 10:27). And in this difficult moment, David turned to the most encouraging person in the universe, his Creator and Friend, and asked, "Lord, what should I do?"

The Lord replied, "Attack, for you will prevail."

God always has an answer for victory even in the middle of defeat. If you want to stay encouraged, don't depend on people or circumstances; rather depend on God 100 percent of the time. He is always in control and always has the right answer. *Nothing* is impossible for Him. And when you hear a word from the Lord, it will give life to your spirit. That is what David knew.

When every possession, significant person, and honor had been stripped from David, he could have responded in anger instead of trust. After all, he knew that he was anointed to be the next king. He certainly was not getting the kind of royal affirmation I might have been looking for if I had experienced that anointing. I would have been looking for events that would cause those I led to give me the esteem I deserve, resources to prepare the way, and growing admiration of the people. I would have searched for indicators that my destiny was just around the corner. I would have expected opportunities to appear, rather than calamities. If I had been in David's position, I know I could have easily fallen into temptation and rage.

That is why David's response to his crisis at Ziklag catches my attention so profoundly. His reaction was opposite of my expectations. Despite the circumstances, David paused to develop and maintain his active, trusting relationship with God. This secret is present not only in what David did but also just as powerfully in what he didn't do. He didn't turn his anger toward God. In his darkest hour, he didn't flee from God; rather, David ran to Him.

Remember, David did not come to Ziklag after having months of positive experiences. No, he came to the city after living more than a year among a godless enemy to God and His covenant people, all because he was forced to flee for his life from his own country. Opportunities for discouragement and bitterness surrounded David. Yet he didn't allow either of these to infect his relationship with God. By every indicator, this experience strengthened David's relationship with God more and more.

Consider the quality of David's communication with God. At Ziklag, David's didn't obsessively ponder over the reasons why this calamity had happened. Instead, he called for the priest Abiathar to help him turn to God for encouragement and strength. That action indicates a living, dynamic relationship. David could live in the world but not be of the world. He could live among the ungodly but not let ungodliness attach itself to him. His response to a crisis was not to retreat, suck his thumb, and whine. It was to get before the living Lord, encourage himself in God, and receive His direction.

The Goodness of God

You must practice trusting God instead of the circumstances, even in tough times, if you want to develop an active, trusting relationship with God. David said it best in the 23rd Psalm: "Yea, though I walk through the valley of the shadow of death, I will fear no evil" (v. 4a). Why would he say this? David told God why:

> For You *are* with me;
> Your rod and Your staff, they comfort me.
> You prepare a table before me in the presence of my enemies;
> You anoint my head with oil;
> My cup runs over (vv. 4b–5).

Not only is God trustworthy, but moreover He never gives up on us. Even if we find ourselves in the valley of the shadow of death, God will not abandon us. Under the gaze of our enemies, God prepares a table before us. In the presence of our worst foes, He anoints our heads with oil. Everything in the natural world around us may scream that God has deserted us, but God is just as near as ever. And He has never stopped working for our good, even in the most desperate of times. He is not the kind of God who will desert us in our bad times. He does not throw us away or reject us when we are going through trouble. He is "a very present help in trouble" (Psalm 46:1).

 Even if we find ourselves in the valley of the shadow of death, God will not abandon us.

It is always easier to see what God has done after the fact than to see what He is doing during the trials. As I write this, I am in my 60s. Now I have no problem seeing how, in my 20s, God was leading me out of the appliance business and into the ministry; how, in my 30s, He was bringing me through every challenge in growing the church and giving birth to our ministry to marriages; and how, in the past 20 years, He has been right in the middle of every step of our continued growth in His plan for our lives and ministry. You, too, can probably look back at numerous evidences of God working on your behalf at times when all you could see was confusion and opposition.

The Value of Controlled Difficulty

Look at just a few of the detailed ways God was actively advancing His plan for David's destiny even during the darkest hours of David's life.

The first thing God did was forge David's character. Being the king of Israel would be no cushy job. It would take a tough man, one strong in his convictions and actions. When Saul was confronted with that challenge, he failed miserably. As a jealous and unsuccessful king, he was in no position to train his anointed successor. David's only hope was that God would ready him. And prepare David He did, in part by allowing David to go through difficult situations. Yet in no instance did God ever lift His protection or let circumstances get out of control.

Look at what was gained by allowing David to flee to the Philistines. Israel's greatest enemy gave a future king inside information about their operations. It was neither comfortable nor glamorous for Israel's king-in-waiting (and hiding!) to have to flee his own country for his life. I'm sure it would have been easy for David to question what God doing at the time. But in those circumstances, Israel's future king saw the underbelly of the enemy and discovered their hidden strategies and weaknesses. Years later, David was the king who destroyed every enemy of Israel, especially the most fearsome of all—the Philistines. That crash course on the enemy paid big dividends later!

What about when David was stripped of everything by the Amalekites? That set the stage for an attack that would restore everything to David and make him a wealthy man. He was able to use that wealth to send gifts to every region of Israel, giving him favor with a torn and divided nation that needed a leader. The events that seemed to mock David's ability to lead at the time were what prepared the nation to recognize and receive him as their new king in the end.

Finally, tough times showed David which men among his followers he could really count on. The worst of times revealed the best in the men who surrounded him. Yes, everyone had joined the plot to stone him as an extension of their grief, and in no way was that a good thing. But when God's plan was set before them, to the man, they laid down their anger and rose up once again to be David's champions. Their true character was revealed in battle. Because David was willing to go through the test to measure his trust in God's faithfulness, he was able to find out who his real leaders were.

Not one insignificant element, not one missed detail, is to be found in these preparations God made for Israel's future ruler. I can imagine David looking back 20 years later and recalling how clearly the hand of God was working in all these events. But in the time of crisis, before he could see the outcome, what mattered was his willingness to trust that God was working behind the scenes.

The Faithfulness of God

In his darkest hour, David encouraged himself by pursuing an active, trusting relationship with God. He said in effect, "Despite what I see, blessed be the name of the Lord. I know You are a good God. Even though I walk through the valley of the shadow of death, You are with me. That may not be what the devil is saying, what my emotions are saying, what the people around me are saying, or what the circumstances are saying. But that is what my heart says and what the Word says, and that makes all the difference."

The greater difficulty is always trusting God's faithfulness in the midst of the challenges. That is when we consciously choose to recall how faithful He has been in the past and how He is working just as hard right now before the outcome is known. There is always something more valuable and more real going on than what we see in the present moment.

This decision to trust does not mean we think God expects us to enjoy bad times. What it does mean is that even when it seems things could get no worse, you have every reason to encourage yourself in Him. You can remember the hard times in the past when your character was forged, your sins were purged, and you learned valuable lessons that could not be taught in the classroom of comfort and ease. The apostle Paul said it this way: "We also glory in tribulations, knowing that tribulation produces perseverance; and perseverance, character; and character, hope" (Romans 5:3–4).

As Joseph in the Old Testament learned through slavery and prison, you can solidify the qualities that equip you to step into your destiny. By remembering God's unbroken record of faithfulness to you, you can rest knowing He is working something beyond what you could imagine. Even in your darkest hour, you can encourage yourself and hold on to the One whose character, promises, and plans never change toward you.

You'll quickly learn to recognize and dismiss the accusing, condemning, negative voice of the enemy that is always trying to convince you that God has given up on you. Even at your worst, he has no grounds. The Bible says, "Where sin abounded, grace abounded much more" (Romans 5:20). God has a destiny for you that cannot be erased—there's nothing you have done and nothing the devil can do to change that. The Lord's voice is always positive toward you, even in correction. In Him there is always hope; there is always help, and there is always light. God is willing to pick you up where you are right now and turn you toward your destiny.

> **God is willing to pick you up where you are right now and turn you toward your destiny.**

Every time something bad happens, don't curl up in defeat and whine. Nurture and practice an active, trusting relationship with God, which means you have to let Him develop in you the qualities you need to lead. David did. It was the first of four secrets that would lead him to staying encouraged on the path to success beyond his wildest imagination.

SECRET #2: A WORD-BASED VIEW OF REALITY

You've probably heard people say these things (and maybe you've even thought such things yourself):

- "Well, I would be encouraged if I just had some money in the bank."
- "I would feel better if my wife would change her attitude toward me."
- "My anxiety would go down if my boss would give me that promotion."

So many times, people tie their encouragement to a situation. When they go through discouraging times, they are waiting to be encouraged when conditions change with their finances, family, or whatever situation challenges them.

David didn't take that position. He didn't wait for things to change to encourage himself. **The second secret of self-encouragement David practiced was a Word-based view of reality.** For you and me, that means believing what the Bible says instead of what our circumstances are trying to tell us.

The reason this secret is so important is that even though David encouraged himself in God and drew reassurance from people around him, nothing changed immediately. But he could still encourage himself because he had made a decision that the only thing he needed for encouragement was to hear from God. David knew he could depend on a word from his heavenly Father. And he knew he had the power to overcome that situation because he had received God's word on it.

We, too, need to settle this issue if we are to stay encouraged in the Lord. We will never rise above our circumstances as long as we are dependent upon the circumstances to tell us what is real.

Two Realities: Spiritual and Physical

Understanding that there is a higher reality does not mean we don't treat circumstances as real. Remember, David was one of those men who "wept until they had no more power to weep" (1 Samuel 30:4). David did not deny the facts of the tragedy. But he did not let the facts serve as the final word on the matter either. He knew there are always two realities at work: the lower, physical reality and the higher, spiritual reality. His hopes and actions were based on what God said about the situation, not simply on what it looked like.

Consider how David grabbed onto the spiritual reality in his circumstances. At Ziklag, whatever was going on behind the scenes spiritually was not initially apparent. David really was the anointed king of Israel—that was the spiritual reality. That fact had not changed one bit, not even in that moment when it looked like he was a failure and about to die at the hands of his own men. But in all truth, David was at the epicenter of God's will, had done nothing wrong, and was about to become king. That was the real truth of the situation. It did not look real, but it was real according to the word of God. When David went before God, the Lord did not correct him; He had nothing negative at all to say about His servant, David. To others, it may have looked as if David had done everything wrong, but he had done nothing wrong in the eyes of God. The truth of the matter existed on a higher plane than what was apparent.

However, the natural facts were there as well. They always are. So what do we do about the other reality that we also live with every day—the physical reality? We don't respond the way the Greek philosopher Plato proposed when he was trying to deal with this issue. Centuries ago, Plato taught a theory that there exists these two realities, which became known as Platonic dualism. He taught that the physical realm is evil, and the spirit realm is good. Plato believed there is a constant battle between the evil physical realm and the good spiritual realm.

Plato's view of the two realities is not the same as the Bible's view. God's Word teaches that the physical realm was created by God, and there is nothing inherently evil about it. The spirit realm also was created by God, but evil forces are at work in it. So evil and good exist in both realms.

When Things Don't Line Up

We can know from the Bible that everything God created is good. We can look at the physical realm and see the beauty of creation, knowing there is nothing wrong with it. At other times, when we look at physical reality, we see things that do not line up with spiritual, or scriptural, reality. We see sick bodies, and we know that is a physical reality. Nevertheless, what should we think about a doctor's report that someone's condition is incurable? Is that real too? It may be real according to natural knowledge and physical laws, but it is not true according to the higher reality. Scripture says, "With God nothing will be impossible" and "The things which are impossible with men are possible with God" (Luke 1:37; 18:27). We could just as easily substitute the word "incurable" for "impossible" in both of those verses. Nothing is incurable with God. When someone makes a general statement that a condition is "impossible" or "incurable" without qualifying it in some way, such as "medically incurable" or "physically impossible, that person fails to acknowledge a higher reality.

People can chooses labels for things according to the limits of human ability, but we should not try to place limitations on God. The facts of the physical realm might be saying, "This is impossible. You will never get out of this mess. It's over, and you are done." Every bit of physical data in front of us could be defying everything God has ever said to us. It could be defying every dream in our hearts and everything we believe about our destinies.

That is the situation that was happening with David. Everything in the natural realm was screaming, "What a joke you are! What an absolute failure! How can you possibly believe you can lead a nation when you cannot even lead the men who have gathered around you?" David neither acknowledged those insinuations nor answered those accusing questions. He had already made a choice—a choice not to accept as final authority what he saw or perceived with his physical senses. Instead he sought a word from God: "God, what do *You* have to say? What do *You* want me to do?" Then God replied, "Attack the Amalekites. You will defeat them."

David took God's word as his reality and said to his men, "Okay, guys, I have the word from God for this situation. It is a good word, not a discouraging word. We are going to attack the Amalekites and win. We are going to recover everything that was taken from us and more." Acting on the higher reality, they not only got their families and possessions back, but they also became rich—and David became king!

It's Your Choice

Today, we know about the encouraging ending to the events at Ziklag. But we should not forget that David did not have that advance knowledge. In the absence of seeing the future, he had to choose which reality he would live by and act upon in the present. He had to decide if he was going to pursue heaven's higher reality until the temporary facts of his current situation turned around and lined up with God's unchanging word or if he was going to fold under the overwhelming circumstances of defeat.

I showed you two Scriptures that declare nothing is impossible with God. But Jesus made this truth even more personal. He said, "I say to you, if you have faith as a mustard seed, you will say to this mountain, 'Move from here to there,' and it will move; and **nothing will be impossible for you**" (Matthew 17:20, emphasis added).

You have the most significant part to play in deciding which reality will be yours. The lower reality is true. It is filled with the facts of every failure, blunder, or mistake you have ever made, and it is shrouded with all the weaknesses, frailties, and sins of the entirety of humanity. It shouts to you that you are bound by your weaknesses and limited by your humanity. It insists that you do not deserve much better than what you've already gotten. It cries for you to cut your losses, lower your vision, and be cautious, lest you ever get your hopes too high.

So which reality is going to come to pass in your life? *The one you believe.* You have to make the choice. They are both the truth, but they are qualitatively different truths. If David had believed the physical reality over the spiritual reality—if he had believed the world over the word—he would have not only felt like a loser and acted like a loser, but also most likely his men would have killed him, and he would have died as a loser. Heaven's reality did not invade the physical, sense-perceived, natural reality that surrounded him until David stood up and not only asked for a word from God but also acted on that word until it prevailed. The reality David chose was the reality that came true. The reality you choose will be the reality that comes true in your life.

 The reality you choose will be the reality that comes true in your life.

Lift Up Your Eyes

In 2 Corinthians 5:7, Paul says, "We walk by faith, not by sight." These two realities—the reality that is perceived by the senses and the reality that is perceived by faith in what God has said—are mutually exclusive.

Every one of us will have to fight this battle every day of our lives. When we look at the world around us right now, the news is discouraging. We hear reports of terrorist acts, hypotheses about the outcomes of global warming, atrocities against children, systematic mass murders of ethnic groups, and threats of deadly worldwide plagues. One reality is that this is a discouraging age in which to live. Another reality is that this is the most exciting time in history to be alive. When the disciples asked Jesus when the end would come, at the end of a list of global calamities, Jesus encouraged those young believers, "When these things begin to happen, look up and lift up your heads, because your redemption draws near" (Luke 21:28).

We are fighting an evil devil and living in a world torn in many ways by darkness, fear, and death. Our challenge is to lift up our heads and set our eyes on a higher reality and a greater expectation. Heaven's truth is "Where sin abounded, grace abounded much more" and "The light shines in the darkness, and the darkness did not comprehend it" (Romans 5:20; John 1:5).

What do you see in front of you right now? You can walk based on what you see, feel, and sense. You can choose to be a victim of circumstances and emotions and live a roller-coaster life of brief highs followed by deep lows. Or you can take the word from God, believe it, act on it, and be an unshakable force on the earth. It will not matter how bad things look; you have a word from God that is more real than anything you see. When everyone else is reeling, feeling discouraged, and giving up, you will be standing fast and firm because you have a word from God. Like David did before it ever looked like he could be king, you'll speak positively, act positively, lead positively, and live positively. And everything God has said concerning you will happen.

You'll turn your back on temporary situations and low-level thinking that would limit you, mock you, and hold you down. And you'll set your sights squarely on the higher reality of the word God has spoken concerning you—a good word He is ready to back up with the Holy Spirit.

God created you in your mother's womb with a destiny you've only begun to imagine. And He believes in you. You are something. You are created in His image; you have His stamp, His imprint, on your life. You are full of God. You're the very temple of His Holy Spirit. And that's the truth. That's the reality taking place in the spiritual realm concerning you right now! Don't you ever doubt that and give the devil the upper hand.

Don't let a Ziklag moment defraud you of your destiny in God!

SECRET #3: A WORSHIPFUL, GOD-FOCUSED MINDSET

David reveals the third secret of self-encouragement in a declaration he makes in Psalm 16:8: "I have set the Lord always before me; because He is at my right hand I shall not be moved." This declaration both raises a question and gives instruction. The question is, would the Lord have gone before David anyway if David had not set the Lord before him?

Actually, the answer is not in where the Lord is but rather where we are. We know the Lord is always with us, whether we set Him before us or not. God is always in our lives. But we don't know He is there until we set Him before us in praise and worship.

It was because David kept the Lord always before him that he could say, "Yea, though I walk through the valley of the shadow of death, I will fear no evil; for You are with me"

(Psalm 23:4). Even though God is with every believer in the valley of the shadow of death or during any other trial of life, many don't walk in the peace and security available to them because they forget He is with them. By not deliberately keeping Him before their faces in worship, people become overwhelmed by the fear of death.

Reality - God = Fear

Did you notice how David described the immediate byproduct of setting the Lord always before him when he said, "I shall not be moved"? We cannot get discouraged, or stay discouraged, when we choose to remember and acknowledge that God is with us. It just isn't possible.

> **We cannot get discouraged, or stay discouraged, when we choose to remember and acknowledge that God is with us.**

When God is before us, there is no problem that's too powerful. He overcomes death. The Lord overcomes debt and family problems. He defeats any enemy. Nothing remains big in God's presence. Everything pales in comparison to Him. David said he would not be moved because he always chose to set the Lord before him. He refused to forget God or to set Him aside.

Is there any situation that is hopeless when God is right there in front of someone? No! To say something is hopeless is to say it is Godless. It is to acknowledge that the devil has erased God from the reality of that particular circumstance or individual. That is the devil's method of operation—he takes an eraser and tries to erase God out of his victim's current reality. Fear is reality minus God.

At the time of the Exodus, when 12 Israelites were sent to spy out the land God had promised His people, 10 of the spies came back with this report: "There we saw the giants (the descendants of Anak came from the giants); and we were like grasshoppers in our own sight, and so we were in their sight" (Numbers 13:33).

I'm sure you realize what happened. The facts of the physical reality became the only thing they could see. These 10 spies reported that the inhabitants were so huge there was no way the Israelites could take the land. And the people believed them. In light of the natural circumstances, they disregarded what God had said. The people even began talking about replacing Moses with leaders who would take them back to Egypt!

Then the other two spies, Joshua and Caleb, gave their report. They did not deny that there were giants in the land, but that was not their main focus. Joshua and Caleb saw God's promise. They saw the abundance of the land just as God had said, and they believed God would keep His word to give that land to them. Joshua and Caleb declared,

> "The land we passed through to spy out is an exceedingly good land. If the Lord delights in us, then He will bring us into this land and give it to us, 'a land which flows with milk and honey.' Only do not rebel against the Lord, nor fear the people of the land, for they are our bread; their protection has departed from them, and the Lord is with us. Do not fear them" (Numbers 14:7–9).

Ten spies compared the giants to themselves, and they became grasshoppers in their own sight. Joshua and Caleb compared the giants to God, and the giants became the grass-hoppers! The 10 fearful men had a Godless view of reality. Because of that fear, they became hopeless. Their hopeless-ness spread throughout the camp, and the Israelites alive at that time did not enter into the land God had promised to them. Joshua and Caleb, however, had a God-centered, worshipful view of life. Had the Israelites listened to them instead of the other spies, the story would have ended very differently.

Psalm 007

This God-centered view is the one we see in many of the psalms of David. And these were not all psalms he wrote during quiet, peaceful days. This fact can be seen in the title attached to Psalm 59: "A Michtam [song or psalm] of David when Saul sent men, and they watched the house in order to kill him." When you read the psalms, don't lose sight of the fact that David wrote some of them during the very worst days of his life.

This true story carries even more suspense than a spy novel or James Bond movie. With the camera pulled back, we can see David's house surrounded by trained government agents on a mission to kill our hero. These assassins were dispatched by King Saul. As the camera zooms inside, we can see their intended victim down on his knees worshipping God. Moving in even closer, we begin to hear what our hero is saying:

> Deliver me from my enemies, O my God;
> Defend me from those who rise up against me.
> Deliver me from the workers of iniquity,
> And save me from bloodthirsty men.
> For look, they lie in wait for my life;
> The mighty gather against me,
> Not for my transgression nor for my sin, O Lord.
> They run and prepare themselves through no fault of mine.
> Awake to help me, and behold!
> You therefore, O Lord God of hosts, the God of Israel,

Awake to punish all the nations;
Do not be merciful to any wicked transgressors.
At evening they return,
They growl like a dog,
And go all around the city.
Indeed, they belch with their mouth;
Swords are in their lips;
For they say, "Who hears?"
But You, O Lord, shall laugh at them;
You shall have all the nations in derision.
I will wait for You, O You his Strength;
For God is my defense;
My God of mercy shall come to meet me;
God shall let me see my desire on my enemies
(Psalm 59:1–10).

Is David aware there is a threat against his life and overwhelming odds against him? Certainly, he is. Is David quaking in fear? Certainly, he is not. Someone other than the enemy troops stands before his face, and when David looks at Him, every enemy looks small: "Look at my enemies, Lord God of the heavenly armies. Listen to their plans to kill me like a pack of dogs." There David is—sitting in his house with the Lord. As he keeps his eyes on God, David sees God laughing at David's enemies. "O Lord, You not only see them; You are laughing at them," he says. "You are going to put into my hands all those who have come against me to kill me."

David wrote this psalm before he fled to the land of the Philistines during the time King Saul was chasing him with the intent to kill him. But the king's strategy failed, because inside a house surrounded by would-be assassins knelt a man who made sure that it was his God and not his troubles set before his face. David reminded himself that God was with him. You can see how impossible it is to discourage someone who has worship as the focus of his mind.

Entering the Peace of God's Presence

God is always there for us, even when we don't worship Him or pray. But when we do not make the effort to praise His name and worship Him, we begin to lose a sense of the reality of His presence and start to react as if He were not there. That is the time when we give the devil an opportunity to drown us in discouragement and torment us with fear.

"Bless the Lord, O my soul,"
the psalmist commanded his mind, will, and emotions in Psalm 103.

> "And all that is within me, *bless* His holy name!
> Bless the Lord, O my soul,
> And forget not all His benefits" (vv. 1–2).

Why should we bless Him? Because the less we praise God and the less we recite His blessings for us, the more likely we are to forget His presence and power in our lives. The more we forget that He is with us, the more discouraged we become.

On the other hand, the more we talk about God and all He has done for us and the more we rehearse His faithfulness and promises, the more encouraged we become and the more we walk by faith. The more we walk by faith, the more we please God and the more we experience His victory in our lives.

Something happens as we choose to keep the unchanging faithfulness of our God before our faces. We remind ourselves that "Jesus Christ *is* the same yesterday, today, and forever" (Hebrews 13:8). A change takes place in our hearts and minds as we set before us the One who is unmoved by the superficial details of the devil's latest attacks. Like David, with God at our right hand, we shall not be moved.

Covered with the Oil of Joy

I've discovered that as I worship in God's presence, not only do I enter into a place of peace, but I also experience the difference between happiness and joy. Isaiah 61, speaking prophetically about the coming ministry of Jesus, says He would come

> To console those who mourn in Zion,
> To give them beauty for ashes,
> The oil of joy for mourning,
> The garment of praise for the spirit of heaviness;
> That they may be called trees of righteousness,
> The planting of the Lord, that He may be glorified (v. 3).

Is that not an amazing thing Jesus came to do? He came to bring consolation to His Church, to His people. He came to give us beauty for ashes, and the oil of joy for mourning.

When rubbed on, oil is an enduring substance; it does not wash off easily with water. That's the way joy behaves as well. Happiness, on the other hand, comes and goes. As the word itself suggests, it is dependent on happenings—happiness depends on our circumstances. Though we could be deliriously happy at one moment, a simple change in our situation five minutes later can send us spiraling into sadness. But joy is abiding. Regardless of what happens, we can have the joy of the Lord. Jesus came to give us the oil of joy, which is also part of the fruit of the Spirit (Galatians 5:22).

During even our darkest days, we can have the joy of the Lord. Joy is the opposite of discouragement. Joy also is a vital weapon of our warfare. Scripture says, "The joy of the Lord is your strength" (Nehemiah 8:10). So when Jesus gives us the oil of joy for our mourning, He is giving us His strength through the Holy Spirit to throw off the things that are discouraging and distracting us.

Put on Your Garment of Praise

And when Jesus gives us the garment of praise, He is giving us the tool for breaking off those things that weigh us down and oppress us. However, as with any other garment, we must put it on to enjoy its full use. We have to purposefully get dressed in praise every morning. As soon as I get up, I have to choose to wear that garment. If I don't, I will not be clothed in praise when I need it, and I will not be able to enjoy the benefit of it. Putting on the garment of praise means I wake up every morning and start praising God first before anything else. Each time I do, the spirit of heaviness is forced to respond—it is forced to leave my presence.

When people only praise God if they *feel* like it, they are missing out on so much! I challenge anyone to praise God and be discouraged at the same time. It simply can't be done. The praise of God is far more powerful than a spirit of discouragement. With a tool of this magnitude at your disposal, getting rid of discouragement is not difficult. In fact, it is impossible to stay discouraged if you choose to praise God in spite of your feelings and circumstances. Voicing the praises of God will change the way you think. It will change the way you feel. If you are sick, you will get healed faster if you praise God for who He is and thank Him for His healing power. If you are discouraged, you find encouragement as you begin to praise the Lord for His goodness and faithfulness.

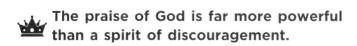

The praise of God is far more powerful than a spirit of discouragement.

255

David was a God-focused, worshipful man. Without ever denying his circumstances, he denied those things the right to have first place in his thinking. He refused to give the situation the ability to move God out of His rightful position before David's face. Because of that mindset, during the worst time in his life, when people were trying to kill him, David was inside his house worshipping and saying in effect, "God, You are laughing at them. You are laughing at my circumstances. You are laughing at my enemies because You already have set in motion Your plan to deliver them into my hands. Thank You, God, for showing me my enemies, for bringing them right here to me!"

When you put on the garment of praise, it will keep you from a spirit of discouragement or depression, no matter who you are or what your circumstances may be. When you have a worshipful, God-focused mindset, you will not be moved, and your enemies will be delivered into your hands. The joy of the Lord is your strength!

SECRET #4: EXPECTATIONS ALIGNED WITH GOD'S REALITY

"Life is tough, and then you die." That bumper sticker has to be one of the saddest I have ever seen. Sadder still is the fact that many people subscribe to this philosophy, even though it directly contradicts the reality God has planned for us. When people adopt a fatalistic attitude, they cut themselves off from the encouragement they need to experience the greatness God put on this earth to achieve. Such people have not discovered the fourth secret to self-encouragement—**the secret of aligning their expectations with God's reality.**

Once again, circumstances looked disastrous for David at Ziklag from several different angles. With the base raided and everything of value taken from David and his followers, any casual onlooker would have to wonder if being anointed as the king of Israel was such a good thing. From the time the prophet Samuel poured the oil of anointing on David's head, his life had been marked by pain and conflict. Still David refused to allow discouragement to take root in his life. He refused to get angry with God.

In the worst circumstance imaginable, David adapted by simply turning and asking, "God, do You want me to fight these people? Do You want me to go ahead?" Free from any fear, self-pity, or anger, he was capable of hearing God's answer: "Yes, go attack them, and you will defeat them."

David didn't waste one minute by becoming preoccupied with the circumstances or by doubting God's plan. David was a realist. And because he thought realistically, he never became overwhelmed. Of course, when we talk about aligning our expectations with reality, we mean aligning them with the higher realm of spiritual reality. We want to see things the way that God sees them.

All too often people fail to align their expectations with God's reality by doing one of two things: they expect victory without opposition, or they expect opposition without victory. When people expect everything to fall into their laps without any difficulty, they are surprised when things don't go smoothly. It disorients them when the path to success is obstructed.

David, however, was not surprised that he had to face challenges and fight to win. Just as surely as he expected victory, he also anticipated opposition—he expected warfare.

What Are Realistic Expectations?

God expects His people to be realists, not only concerning His faithfulness to the promises He has given them, but also to the opposition that will come against His Word. "In the world you will have tribulation," Jesus said; "but be of good cheer, I have overcome the world" (John 16:33). He did not say be cheerful about the tribulation. He said rejoice in the reality that He has overcome the world. The apostle John tells us, "Every child of God defeats this evil world, and we achieve this victory through our faith" (1 John 5:4 NLT).

Then what is the realistic expectation of a joyful, overcoming believer? It is to expect difficulty, followed by victory. If you want to live your life without disappointment, expect difficulty followed by victory.

First the Difficulty

Yes, you are going to succeed and walk in the blessing God has promised, but in the process, you are going to have to fight a battle. No life demonstrates this truth more than that of the apostle Paul. He had to endure a tremendous amount of difficulty to be the person God called him to be. Paul wrote about aligning expectations with reality this way: "We also glory in tribulations, knowing that tribulation produces perseverance; and perseverance, character; and character, hope. Now hope does not disappoint, because the love of God has been poured out in our hearts by the Holy Spirit who was given to us" (Romans 5:3–5). Tribulation means suffering and distress. Paul experienced exactly what Jesus said: "In the world you will have tribulation; but be of good cheer, I have overcome the world" (John 16:33).

What does tribulation produce? Disappointment and defeat? Not for the believer who knows what is on the other side of life's challenges. "Tribulation produces perseverance," Paul wrote. Perseverance is spiritual and emotional toughness—what the dictionary defines as "the ability to continue a course of action in spite of difficulty or opposition."

In turn, perseverance produces the character of God in us. And the character of God in us establishes hope that we can get through this—and that we can get through anything.

The result is spiritual and emotional toughness. God wants a people ready for warfare. Nowhere in Scripture do we find God promising that we will walk in His blessings and experience success without challenges. Apparently, some people were just as surprised at this experience in the apostle Peter's day as they are in ours. So he addressed it head-on: "Beloved, do not think it strange concerning the fiery trial which is to try you, as though some strange thing happened to you; but rejoice to the extent that you partake of Christ's sufferings, that when His glory is revealed, you may also be glad with exceeding joy" (1 Peter 4:12–13).

Peter was apparently writing to a group of saints who were overwhelmed by the fact that they were going through some troubles. He asked why they were so surprised that they were encountering opposition on the way to their victory. He wanted to know why they were acting like going through trials was a strange thing. Trials are going to happen. What the overcoming believer will do is expect them, glory in them when they come, and let God have His way. The person who becomes discouraged and stays that way is the one who started with unrealistic expectations—the one who expected victory without any difficulty or battle. Often that person is the one who will fall the longest and hardest.

Then the Victory

An even worse mindset is held by a second group of believers. This is the group represented by the bumper sticker I mentioned earlier: "Life is tough, and then you die." Things always get worse, they think; nothing ever improves. Even in the best situations, people such as these refuse to be encouraged. They expect the rug to be pulled out from under them at any moment. In discussing secret number three, we discovered that people often tie their encouragement to their circumstances. But this group of believers doesn't even do that. They refuse to be encouraged at all! Even in the best of times, they are thinking and talking about the worst scenario that could happen.

A person of this type expects difficulty without victory. There could be any number of reasons for this expectation. They may have really taken a beating in life. Perhaps they experienced devastation of one kind or another—abandonment, financial failure, divorce, abuse, or whatever it may be. To accommodate their disappointments, they vowed never again to expect anything good to happen, reasoning that if they did not expect it, then they would not be disappointed.

Sadly, their philosophy is totally ineffective as a way to isolate themselves from the disappointment they so desperately seek to escape. Choosing never to expect anything brings a chronic state of disappointment. That's because every person has a God-given dream in his or her heart. When that dream is constantly frustrated, that person can never be the person God created him or her to be. That person can never truly be happy. Scripture warns, "Hope deferred makes the heart sick" (Proverbs 13:12).

Victory Is Your Birthright

Those who refuse to expect any dream or desire of their heart to come to pass are those who have given up the birthright of victory Jesus revealed to Peter in Matthew 16: "You are Peter, and on this rock I will build My church, and the gates of Hades shall not prevail against it" (v. 18). Not Peter himself, but his faith, immovable in the face of any opposition, is the foundation of the Church and the irresistible force no gates of hell can withstand.

Victory is your birthright. Yes, you will have trouble along the way. But the troubles and trials are temporary. They are not the lasting part of your reality. They are not what will remain in the end. Victory will. Victory is your birthright because Jesus has overcome the world.

> ♛ **Victory is your birthright because Jesus has overcome the world.**

If you want to see who walks in the reality God has declared for His people, look at the next words Jesus spoke to Peter: "I will give you the keys of the kingdom of heaven, and whatever you bind on earth will be bound in heaven, and whatever you loose on earth will be loosed in heaven" (v. 19).

Your choice is to roll over and play dead when you experience hardships and challenges in life or to be the person God uses to enforce heaven's reality on this earth. As a person who has been reborn and made a new creature through faith in Christ, you have been given authority in the affairs of this earth. But you have to use it.

"I have given you authority to trample on snakes and scorpions and to overcome all the power of the enemy; nothing will harm you," Jesus declared to all who would follow Him (Luke 10:19 NIV). Will you experience the daily challenges of a world infected with the hurts, disappointments, and temporary setbacks of the devil's deception? Yes. But that is not the end of the story. For those who will take it, Jesus has given the authority to enforce the enemy's defeat. He said, "I give you the power over all the camp of the enemy, and if you use that power, you are not going to be harmed." In Romans 8:37 the apostle Paul said it this way: "In all these things we are more than conquerors through Him who loved us."

Difficulties are part of a realistic expectation about life. You can expect every important thing that you ever do to be opposed tooth-and-nail by the devil. He is going to fight you for your marriage, your children, your ministry—for every single thing God will ever give you in this life.

That fight will be overwhelming for the group caught off guard by the difficulties—the ones who believed they could experience victory without any opposition. And it will be overwhelming to those who have stopped expecting anything out of life but a fight—those who have settled on the fact that they will continually get the stuffing beat out of them. Neither group has a realistic expectation with which to stir up self-encouragement. Neither group realizes they have a choice. But for those who know what God has said and know they have a choice, the good news is this: though it will be a fight, you can beat the enemy 100 percent of the time!

Great Expectations and Work Ethic

I don't know of any place where we can see the value of realistic expectations more clearly than in the battle for our marriages. The number one cause for divorce is not a lack of communication, sexual frustrations, financial difficulties, or problems with children. *It's disappointment.* Couples get married and then expect to live happily ever after without any challenges. They think they have found the perfect soul mate, and everything is going to be great after they say, "I do." But when they find out that they did not marry the perfect mate (there are none!), and things get difficult (they always do!), their dreams crumble and die because of broken hearts and unrealistic expectations. That is when the devil sneaks up and says, *You married the wrong person. Your real soul mate is on the Internet somewhere. You need to get online and find them.*

262

How do we counter that disappointment? Not by lowering our expectations of marriage but by being realistic about our expectations. Research has proven that the greatest marriages are between two people who have the highest expectations and the greatest work ethic combined.

Tough-minded dreamers succeed in marriage. Others do not. The best marriages are between people who say, "We want our marriage to be like this. We want to reach these goals. We want our children to realize these things about their potential in God." But in addition to having high expectations, successful couples link their dreams to a work ethic that says, "We are going to have to work hard at this. It is going to take a lot of praying and some sacrifice. We know the devil is going to fight us, but these are our dreams, and we are destined to overcome everything he throws at us. We will not give up."

The best marriages are between two people who go through hell together and come out on the other side having fought for their marriage, having fought for their children, having fought for their businesses and ministries, and who never give up until they have in hand the victory that was theirs in the One who has overcome the world!

It's Worth the Fight

One reason David never gave in to discouragement is he never was surprised at the fight. He aligned his expectations with reality, while living with his sword at hand at all times, ready for the fight. David was no robot. When the Amalekites had taken everything he had, he cried—he had human emotions. Then David got control of himself, encouraged himself in God, and took everything back.

Understand this: what God gives to you is yours. If God gave it to you, and the devil tries to take it away, you will have a fight on your hands. But it is a fight you will win if you refuse to lay down and let the devil have it. You are a winner. You have God's authority, the name and blood of Jesus, and the Word of God, which is the sword of the Spirit. Whether you know it or not, every demon of hell is afraid of you and dreads the day you will wake up to the authority and power you have in the anointing of Jesus Christ.

No wonder those demons are going to fight against you. You are a real threat to them and their leader. You are part of the only force on earth that can stop the devil and his minions. You are part of the Church whose advance not even the gates of hell can prevail against.

This reality is so terrifying to the devil that he's doing everything he can to prolong his deception. He is trying to make us into a bunch of losers by getting us to believe something that is not true. The devil is trying to push us into the camp that believes life is just going to hand us everything without a battle or into the group that believes there is always going to be a battle but never be a victory.

Wake up to what the devil already knows—we have been given the authority and power to take back everything he has stolen from us. Yes, there is going to be a battle, but it is one we will win because our God has overcome the devil.

Victory Without Battle—a Tormenting Fantasy

There was a time when I didn't know that there is no victory without battle. I have never been naturally cynical; I do not believe that there is going to be trouble without victory. But at one time, I was in the other camp. I had that unrealistic dreamer's mentality that my victories would come without opposition, and it almost cost us our marriage. I was on the threshold of divorce before I realized what Karen already knew—that I was going to have to fight for my marriage. But when Karen and I began to fight for our marriage together, we won. And our prize is the marriage we always dreamed of having.

Not only did we win the battle for our marriage, but we also won the battle for our children. In Proverbs 22:6 we are instructed and promised,

> Train up a child in the way he should go,
> And when he is old he will not depart from it.

If you are a parent, then you are going to have to fight for your children. You will have some tough times along the way. And it will seem that, just when you get everything right, they will get older and present a new set of challenges. Have you noticed that? You finally get the "terrible twos" mastered, and they turn three. Before you know it, they have entered puberty. Then they are teenagers with a whole new set of challenges. They are constantly changing.

There is some truth in what one person said about success in parenting: you do not know how well you have done as a parent until your children turn 30. The proverb just quoted says, *"When he is old* he will not depart from it." It does not say the battles will cease. It does not promise that there won't be some discouraging moments.

A mother can be especially susceptible to discouragement when she is having trouble with her children. The devil will take a snapshot of a disappointing moment and rub her face in it to make her think she is a terrible mother because her children are not perfect. The fact is, you can be the best parent in the world and still face struggles with your children. There never was a child who dropped out of heaven perfect, never presenting a problem for his or her parents. Perfect children simply do not exist. To have children that are good, accept the fact you are going to have to battle.

The Stamina to Stand and Win

What is true about fighting for our marriages and families is true with all of life. My greatest disappointments in the pastorate, in the MarriageToday ministry, or in any other significant area of my life have been from not expecting the battle.

When we started the MarriageToday television ministry, someone commented, "Once you go on TV, in about six months you will start seeing a positive cash flow." That contributed to wildly unrealistic expectations on my part.

Now MarriageToday is going to more than 90 million households in America and over 200 countries worldwide and is financially viable. But for the first three to four years, we fasted and prayed several times about shutting it down. We did this, not because anything radically unusual was happening, but simply because our expectations were so unrealistic. We had thought that, just because we were on television, suddenly a bunch of people would start supporting the ministry. We had to come to the realization that some of our expectations were wrong.

During one of those early, desperate days, I sat down with John Hagee, a pastor who has a television ministry and is one of the kindest men I have ever met. I was trying to figure out how to survive another week. I picked his brain, asking every question I could possibly think to ask. *How do you do this? How do you do that?* Then, after about 30 minutes, he smiled at me and said, "Jimmy, I can answer some of your questions. But the bottom line is, you are just going to have to take some of your own licks on the road to success!"

In other words, he was telling me that my victory would not come without a fight. That was not something I wanted to hear. I remember thinking, *I rebuke that in the name of*

Jesus! But if you listen to the testimonies of the success of any ministry, you will hear how they all fought for their existence—and won. What they learned in those battles has kept them encouraged and on the front line of the devil's defeat.

Stop thinking you are going to be the first person who will waltz in and win your destiny in God without a fight. That is not going to happen. But when you engage the enemy and walk through whatever is between you and your dream, you will meet Jesus in the fire.

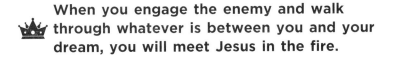 **When you engage the enemy and walk through whatever is between you and your dream, you will meet Jesus in the fire.**

You will forever settle the reality that your God is overwhelmingly greater than any other force on this earth. He is so overwhelmingly superior to anything or anybody that you'll know there is nothing to be fearful of—*ever!*

Part Nine

THE WILLING SERVANT

Lesson 10

USE YOUR FREE WILL TO SERVE THE LORD

DAVID'S LIFE IS a gold mine of valuable lessons in what to do and what not to do when stepping into our dreams and callings in life. He didn't become great because of some inborn superiority or special endowment by God. He became great because he chose to focus on God, be a worshipper of God, and act on God's faithfulness to champion the cause of those who trust the Lord. David purposed to set God always before him, no matter the circumstances. David surrendered his free will to God to serve Him. That is the ultimate secret of David's success in becoming great. And that is not true only for David.

This list of David's actions demonstrates the tenth truth about greatness: great people use their God-given free will to serve the Lord. Greatness isn't for a select few. All of us are destined for greatness if we choose to surrender to God and His plan for our lives. This is the issue that sets truly great people apart from the rest.

Given enough time, I could have focused on other great people in the Bible. Not just men—like Abraham, Joseph, the prophets, and the disciples—but also women like Deborah the judge, who led Israel's army in victory over the Canaanite army, and Jael, the one who bravely killed the commander of that enemy army in the days after Joshua. I could write about Esther, who courageously saved her nation from a plot to destroy her people through ethnic cleansing. And the life of the businesswoman Lydia, in whose home the church at Philippi was started, would make an interesting study. The call to greatness is not for just a select few. It is for every man, woman, boy, and girl created by God and given the privilege and responsibility of living on this earth in the power of His Son.

What I pray you have realized in this study is that no Bible hero—David included—was any less human than you or me. That should be an encouragement to each of us that achieving greatness is about God and not about us. It is about being willing to serve God, believing in what He has promised, and being quick repenters when we mess up.

THE BATTLE FOR GREATNESS

Businesses, governments, financial institutions, ministries, medical facilities, educational institutions, athletes and teams, the entertainment industry—every arena of influence on the earth—are calling for godly leaders. Families, communities, and marketplaces are crying out too.

And God is calling you to answer.

He is calling you to be a leader in your family, job, business, church, civic organizations, and government bodies. He is calling for you to stand up among other leaders. He is calling you to make a difference for defenseless, disregarded, and discarded people. In every role God is calling you to step into, He has already provided and prepared you completely and is actively working on your behalf.

God's plans are always and only for your good: "'I know the plans I have for you,' declares the Lord, 'plans to prosper you

and not to harm you, plans to give you hope and a future'"
(Jeremiah 29:11 NIV). He issued His call on your life before
you were born—it's a call shaped in your DNA. God says of
you the same thing He said of the prophet Jeremiah:

> Before I formed you in the womb I knew you,
> before you were born I set you apart;
> I appointed you as a prophet to the nations
> (Jeremiah 1:5 NIV).

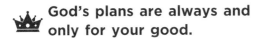 **God's plans are always and only for your good.**

Let there be no doubt about it: your heavenly Father
uniquely and purposefully created you like no other person
on earth. The way David lived shows us he clearly believed
that about his own life. And this psalm he wrote beautifully
expresses that truth when he says of God:

> You made all the delicate, inner parts of my body
>> And knit me together in my mother's womb.
> Thank you for making me so wonderfully complex!
>> Your workmanship is marvelous—how well I know it.
> You watched me as I was being formed in utter seclusion,
>> As I was woven together in the dark of the womb.
> You saw me before I was born.
>> Every day of my life was recorded in your book.
> Every moment was laid out
>> Before a single day had passed.
> How precious are your thoughts about me, O God.
>> They cannot be numbered!
> I can't even count them;
>> They outnumber the grains of sand!
>> (Psalm 139:13–18 NLT)

The truth is, God planned for you from before the foundation of the world, chose the time when you would be born, and was intimately and intricately involved in every detail of your creation. He has never stopped thinking about you or working on your behalf to assure that you have every opportunity to see His promises and plans fulfilled in your life.

There are things He has called and equipped you to do that no one else can do exactly like you. You fill a unique place in your family and your world. Even as you are still finding out who you are becoming, never forget that God has given His best for you and equipped you to bring His best to your world.

Walking out God's plan for your best is not going to come without opposition, especially when you become a leader and begin helping others realize their greatness in God. Just know that the enemy is going to aim hard-hitting questions your way. Either from your own thoughts or from those around you, you'll be faced with questions like these:

Just who do you think you are?

With the obvious weaknesses in your life, what makes you think you are qualified to lead?

My advice? When these questions come, don't bat an eye. Whether you are looking at yourself in the mirror or facing another person, be quick to say, "It's not about me; it's about the God in me who has made me who I am and called me with His unique calling. Christ in me is my qualification. His righteousness is my authority, and His Word is my reality. In Him I am called to enforce the devil's defeat and bring heaven on earth!"

If you are at a point in your life where it appears everything is going wrong and nothing is lining up with the destiny you were created to fulfill, don't let that surprise you! Remember, we have talked about numerous instances in David's life that could have cast doubt on his destiny—he experienced his own failings, family dysfunction, opposition from others, and everything in between. Also remember how that right before David was to become king, the devil attacked him the hardest. He'll try the same tactic on you. He'll do his level best to keep you from stepping into what God has in store for you.

Now, this is very important. Right in the middle of all that demonic opposition, God wants you to realize that He is always and in every way more powerful than the devil. He wants you to rest assured that even in the worst circumstances, He will never give up on you, and He is always there to encourage you when you will turn to and depend on Him.

You were created uniquely and completely by God with a capacity and a desire to fulfill God's purpose for your life ... not too early, nor too late, but right on time.

THE RIGHT STUFF

Satan's worst fear is that you will wake up to who you are in Christ. His greatest nightmare happens when you discover that you are wired for battle and have been given powerful weapons of warfare to enforce his defeat at the cross. No wonder he works so hard to get you to believe you don't have the right stuff to succeed!

The devil will never stop trying, but he's too late. By now you have seen that the real issue is neither how many ways you could fail nor how many reasons you cannot succeed in your own strength. The real issue is how impossible it is for you to fail in God. There are no impossible situations for Him: "The things which are impossible with men are possible with God" (Luke 18:27). Because of that truth, there are no limits to what you can accomplish when you speak and act in faith on what God has promised. "If you have faith ... nothing will be impossible for you," Jesus said (Matthew 17:20).

You cannot be defeated if you will choose, like David did, to dedicate yourself to God and trust in Him in the good times and bad. King David is an example to all of us that common people called from the sheepfolds can do great things if we will keep our hearts turned toward God and keep seeking Him. You've got what it takes! Just like David, you are destined for greatness. Enter the battlefield and fulfill your destiny in God.

Just like David, you are destined for greatness.

Appendix I

LEADER GUIDE

LEADER GUIDE

The *I Am David* Leader Guide is designed to help you lead your small group or class through the *I Am David* book. Use this guide for a life-changing, interactive experience.

BEFORE YOU MEET

- Ask God to prepare the hearts and minds of the people in your group. Ask Him to show you how to encourage each person to integrate the principles they discover through reading this book and group discussion into their daily lives.

- Before the meeting, read the chapter you will be discussing and familiarize yourself with that chapter's discussion and activation questions.

- Plan how much time you'll give to each portion of your meeting (see the suggested schedule below).

SUGGESTED SMALL GROUP SCHEDULE

1. **Engage** and **Recap** (5 Minutes)

2. **Read** (20 Minutes)

3. **Talk** (25 Minutes)

4. **Pray** (10 minutes)

KEY TIPS FOR THE LEADER

• Generate participation and discussion.

• Resist the urge to teach. The goal is for great conversation that leads to discovery.

• Ask open-ended questions—questions that can't be answered with "yes" or "no" (e.g., "What do you think about that?" rather than "Do you agree?")

• When a question arises, ask the group for their input first, instead of immediately answering it yourself.

• Be comfortable with silence. If you ask a question and no one responds, rephrase the question and wait for a response. Your primary role is to create an environment where people feel comfortable to be themselves and participate, not to provide the answers to all of their questions.

• Ask the group to pray for each other from week to week, especially about key issues that arise during your group time. This is how you begin to build authentic community and encourage spiritual growth within the group.

KEYS TO A DYNAMIC SMALL GROUP

RELATIONSHIPS

Meaningful, encouraging relationships are the foundation of a dynamic small group. Teaching, discussion, worship, and prayer are important elements of a group meeting, but the depth of each element is often dependent upon the depth of the relationships among members.

AVAILABILITY

Building a sense of community within your group requires members to prioritize their relationships with one another. This means being available to listen, care for one another, and meet each other's needs.

MUTUAL RESPECT

Mutual respect is shown when members value each other's opinions (even when they disagree) and are careful never to put down or embarrass others in the group (including their spouses, who may or may not be present).

OPENNESS

A healthy small group environment encourages sincerity and transparency. Members treat each other with grace in areas of weakness, allowing each other room to grow.

CONFIDENTIALITY

To develop authenticity and a sense of safety within the group, each member must be able to trust that things discussed within the group will not be shared outside the group.

SHARED RESPONSIBILITY

Group members will share the responsibility of group meetings by using their God-given abilities to serve at each gathering. Some may greet, some may host, some may teach, etc. Ideally, each person should be available to care for others as needed.

SENSITIVITY

Dynamic small groups are born when the leader consistently seeks and is responsive to the guidance of the Holy Spirit, following His leading throughout the meeting as opposed to sticking to the "agenda." This guidance is especially important during the discussion and ministry time.

FUN!

Dynamic small groups take the time to have fun. Create an atmosphere for fun and be willing to laugh at yourself every now and then!

Appendix II

STUDY GUIDE

JOIN THE BATTLE

INTRODUCTION

Every person has a calling to greatness, and the best years of your life will be those spent on the battlefield serving the Lord. David's greatest years were those when he was faithful to his calling. However, when he decided to stay home, dysfunction and destruction entered, hurting both him and his family.

KEY THOUGHT

You won't discover your true greatness until you find it on the battlefield.

KEY SCRIPTURES

2 Samuel 11:1, 3–5

It happened in the spring of the year, at the time when kings go out *to battle*, that David sent Joab and his servants with him, and all Israel; and they destroyed the people of Ammon and besieged Rabbah. But David remained at

Jerusalem.... David sent and inquired about the woman. And *someone* said, "*Is* this not Bathsheba, the daughter of Eliam, the wife of Uriah the Hittite?" Then David sent messengers, and took her; and she came to him, and he lay with her, for she was cleansed from her impurity; and she returned to her house. And the woman conceived; so she sent and told David, and said, "I *am* with child."

2 Samuel 12:8–11

I gave you your master's house and your master's wives into your keeping, and gave you the house of Israel and Judah. And if *that had been* too little, I also would have given you much more! Why have you despised the commandment of the Lord, to do evil in His sight? You have killed Uriah the Hittite with the sword; you have taken his wife to be your wife, and have killed him with the sword of the people of Ammon. Now therefore, the sword shall never depart from your house, because you have despised Me, and have taken the wife of Uriah the Hittite to be your wife. Thus says the Lord: "Behold, I will raise up adversity against you from your own house."

Ephesians 6:10–17

Finally, my brethren, be strong in the Lord and in the power of His might. Put on the whole armor of God, that you may be able to stand against the wiles of the devil. For we do not wrestle against flesh and blood, but against principalities, against powers, against the rulers of the darkness of this age, against spiritual hosts of wickedness in the heavenly places. Therefore take up the whole armor of God, that you may be able to withstand in the evil day, and having done all, to stand.

Stand therefore, having girded your waist with truth, having put on the breastplate of righteousness, and having shod your feet with the preparation of the gospel of peace; above all, taking the shield of faith with which you will be able to quench all the fiery darts of the wicked one. And take the helmet of salvation, and the sword of the Spirit, which is the word of God.

DISCUSSION

• Explain this statement: *Every person ever born was wired for war.*

• What made David such a great warrior for so many years?

• What are the three lies of retreat that keep us from the battlefield? How have you experienced these in your life?

ACTIVATION

• Have you ever tried to cover up a sin? What were the results?

• Ask yourself, "Am I spending my time on the battlefield or on the rooftop?"

• Ask God to give you the courage to stay on the battlefield, no matter how often the enemy comes against you.

TAKE RESPONSIBILITY FOR YOUR MISTAKES

INTRODUCTION

Everyone makes mistakes. What determines whether you become a true champion is what you do about your mistakes. David made some terrible choices, but he always ran to God and admitted his sins. God forgave David, and He will forgive you too.

KEY THOUGHT

Every great person takes responsibility for his or her mistakes and becomes great through them.

KEY SCRIPTURES

Psalm 51:1–4

Have mercy upon me, O God,
According to Your lovingkindness;
According to the multitude of Your tender mercies,
Blot out my transgressions.

Wash me thoroughly from my iniquity,
And cleanse me from my sin.
For I acknowledge my transgressions,
And my sin is always before me.
Against You, You only, have I sinned,
And done this evil in Your sight—
That You may be found just when You speak,
And blameless when You judge.

DISCUSSION

• How did Adam and Eve respond when they sinned?

• How is Jesus the ultimate example of responsibility? What are some of the ways you can follow His example?

• What was David's first mistake in the incident with Bathsheba? Against whom did he sin?

ACTIVATION

• How do you react when you make a mistake?

• Recognize that when you sin, it is always against God even if it is also against others. Pray, "God, please help me admit my sins openly and honestly before You."

• Thank the Lord for His amazing forgiveness and grace.

RISE ABOVE THE PAIN OF THE PAST

INTRODUCTION

Every person has been hurt in one way or another. David was great on the battlefield, but his past was filled with pain from being ignored by his father, scorned by his brother, and rejected by his "boss," King Saul. Because David did not deal with his pain, he was much less successful as a father and husband than he was as a military leader.

KEY THOUGHT

Every great person rises above the pain of the past to reach his or her God-given destiny.

KEY SCRIPTURES

1 Samuel 16:10–11

Thus Jesse made seven of his sons pass before Samuel. And Samuel said to Jesse, "The Lord has not chosen these." And Samuel said to Jesse, "Are all the young men here?" Then he said, "There remains yet the youngest, and there he is, keeping the sheep."

And Samuel said to Jesse, "Send and bring him. For we will not sit down till he comes here." So he sent and brought him in. Now he was ruddy, with bright eyes, and good-looking. And the Lord said, "Arise, anoint him; for this is the one!" Then Samuel took the horn of oil and anointed him in the midst of his brothers; and the Spirit of the Lord came upon David from that day forward.

Ephesians 4:26–27 TLB

If you are angry, don't sin by nursing your grudge. Don't let the sun go down with you still angry—get over it quickly; for when you are angry, you give a mighty foothold to the devil.

Philippians 3:13–15

Brethren, I do not count myself to have apprehended; but one thing I do, forgetting those things which are behind and reaching forward to those things which are ahead, I press toward the goal for the prize of the upward call of God in Christ Jesus.

Therefore let us, as many as are mature, have this mind; and if in anything you think otherwise, God will reveal even this to you.

DISCUSSION

• What are the three wrong substitutes for healing?

• Explain this statement: *God's ability to talk with you about your future is limited by how much you will allow Him to talk about your past.*

• How is Paul an example of the right way to deal with your past?

ACTIVATION

• In what areas of life have you felt the most rejection?

• Ask yourself, "Do I respond to rejection like David or like Paul?"

• Admit your pain to God and ask Him to end it through Jesus.

PAY THE PRICE TO BE A WORSHIPPER

INTRODUCTION

David is often remembered for being a poet, shepherd, warrior, and king, but he was first and foremost a worshipper. He introduced praise and worship to Israel, and his throne was established by God as the permanent throne of Israel. We should follow David's example and worship the Lord with all our heart, soul, and strength, regardless of what those around us might think.

KEY THOUGHT

Every great person is a worshipper of God and pays a price to be so.

KEY SCRIPTURES

Isaiah 9:6–7

Unto us a Child is born,
Unto us a Son is given;

And the government will be upon His shoulder.
And His name will be called
Wonderful, Counselor, Mighty God,
Everlasting Father, Prince of Peace.
Of the increase of *His* government and peace
There will be no end,
Upon the throne of David and over His kingdom,
To order it and establish it with judgment and justice
From that time forward, even forever.

Acts 15:16–17

"After this I will return
And will rebuild the tabernacle of David, which has fallen down;
I will rebuild its ruins,
And I will set it up;
So that the rest of mankind may seek the Lord,
Even all the Gentiles who are called by My name,
Says the Lord who does all these things."

Psalm 107:20

He sent His word and healed them,
And delivered them from their destructions.

DISCUSSION

• What are the four distinguishing characteristics of David's reign as king?

• How was David's tabernacle different from Moses and Solomon's places of worship?

• Define false worship.

ACTIVATION

• Do you think God would describe you as a person after His own heart? Why or why not?

• Ask yourself, "Is any part of me spiritually sterile?"

• Commit to worshipping God in the way He desires.

BE POSITIVE REGARDLESS
OF THE CIRCUMSTANCES

INTRODUCTION

Any soldier in Israel could have done what David did if he had thought the way David thought. David was a faith-focused thinker. He believed the reward for defeating Goliath was greater than the risk, and he was willing to fight the enemy because he knew whose side God was on.

KEY THOUGHT

Every great person thinks in a positive, God-focused manner, regardless of the circumstances.

KEY VERSES

2 Samuel 23:20–21

Benaiah was the son of Jehoiada, the son of a valiant man from Kabzeel, who had done many deeds. He had killed two lion-like heroes of Moab. He also had gone down and killed a lion in the midst of a pit on a snowy day. And he killed an Egyptian, a spectacular man. The Egyptian had a spear in his hand; so he went down to him with a staff, wrested the spear out of the Egyptian's hand, and killed him with his own spear.

1 Chronicles 20:6–7

Yet again there was war at Gath, where there was a man of great stature, with twenty-four fingers and toes, six on each hand and six on each foot; and he also was born to the giant. So when he defied Israel, Jonathan the son of Shimea, David's brother, killed him.

DISCUSSION

- What were the rewards for the man who defeated Goliath?

- What are the four characteristics of the way winners think?

- Circumcision was a sign of what to the people of Israel?

ACTIVATION

- Who are some mighty men or women of the faith that you admire?

- Ask yourself, "Do I think like a winner, or do I let fear direct my thoughts?"

- Pray, "Lord, please help me change the way I think."

SUBMIT TO GOD'S AUTHORITY AND TO THOSE HE DELEGATES

INTRODUCTION

David was not perfect, but he was a man after God's heart. He constantly submitted to authority, even when King Saul was trying to kill him. God's kingdom is one of order and authority, and Jesus' ministry is a perfect example of the principle of submission.

KEY THOUGHT

Every great person is exalted by God as he or she humbly submits to God's direct authority and to His delegated human authority on earth.

KEY SCRIPTURES

1 Samuel 15:10–11

Now the word of the Lord came to Samuel, saying, "I greatly regret that I have set up Saul *as* king, for he has turned back from following Me, and has not performed My commandments." And it grieved Samuel, and he cried out to the Lord all night.

Luke 2:48–52

So when they saw Him, they were amazed; and His mother said to Him, "Son, why have You done this to us? Look, Your father and I have sought You anxiously."

And He said to them, "Why did you seek Me? Did you not know that I must be about My Father's business?" But they did not understand the statement which He spoke to them.

Then He went down with them and came to Nazareth, and was subject to them, but His mother kept all these things in her heart. And Jesus increased in wisdom and stature, and in favor with God and men.

Romans 13:4–7

For he is God's minister to you for good. But if you do evil, be afraid; for he does not bear the sword in vain; for he is God's minister, an avenger to execute wrath on him who practices evil. Therefore you must be subject, not only because of wrath but also for conscience' sake. For because of this you also pay taxes, for they are God's ministers attending continually to this very thing. Render therefore to all their due: taxes to whom taxes are due, customs to whom customs, fear to whom fear, honor to whom honor.

DISCUSSION

- Why did God remove King Saul from the throne of Israel?

- What are the seven truths about submission?

- Why is submission so important for parents to teach to their children?

ACTIVATION

- Is submission a difficult topic for you? Do you struggle with authority?

- Thank the Lord for placing godly leaders in your life.

- Determine to honor and submit to God's direct and delegated authority today.

ADMIT WEAKNESSES AND BECOME ACCOUNTABLE TO OTHERS

INTRODUCTION

David was not a perfect man, but he recognized his areas of weakness and turned to God for help. In order for people to become successful, they must recognize that they have been divinely disabled. Only through the help of God and godly people can we achieve true greatness.

KEY THOUGHT

Every great person is incomplete in his or her giftings, personality, and intellect.

KEY SCRIPTURES

Hebrews 13:17

Obey those who rule over you, and be submissive, for they watch out for your souls, as those who must give account.

Let them do so with joy and not with grief, for that would be unprofitable for you.

Proverbs 11:14

Where *there is* no counsel, the people fall;
But in the multitude of counselors *there is* safety.

2 Corinthians 12:7–10

And lest I should be exalted above measure by the abundance of the revelations, a thorn in the flesh was given to me, a messenger of Satan to buffet me, lest I be exalted above measure. Concerning this thing I pleaded with the Lord three times that it might depart from me. And He said to me, "My grace is sufficient for you, for My strength is made perfect in weakness." Therefore most gladly I will rather boast in my infirmities, that the power of Christ may rest upon me. Therefore I take pleasure in infirmities, in reproaches, in needs, in persecutions, in distresses, for Christ's sake. For when I am weak, then I am strong.

DISCUSSION

- What was David's secret to success as a leader?

- What are the five areas of dependence that helped David become a great leader?

- What are two major barriers to honest dependence?

ACTIVATION

- Do you, like David, have psalms in your life? Or are you more like King Saul?

- Examine your heart and ask yourself, "How do I deal with my weaknesses?"

- Ask God to bring godly friends and leaders into your life.

DEPEND ON GOD AND GIVE HIM THE GLORY

INTRODUCTION

Every great person must ask, "How much can God bless me before I use it against Him?" David strayed from his loyalty to God by trying to measure his own greatness, instead of recognizing that it was God who had blessed him. We must choose to reject to reject the whisper of pride and remember who our true Source is.

KEY THOUGHT

Great men and women are those who humbly depend upon God and give Him the praise and glory He deserves.

KEY VERSES

James 4:7–10

Therefore submit to God. Resist the devil and he will flee from you. Draw near to God and He will draw near to you. Cleanse your hands, you sinners; and purify your hearts, you double-minded. Lament and mourn and weep! Let your laughter be turned to mourning and your joy to gloom. Humble yourselves in the sight of the Lord, and He will lift you up.

James 4:7–10

Likewise you younger people, submit yourselves to your elders. Yes, all of you be submissive to one another, and be clothed with humility, for
"God resists the proud,
But gives grace to the humble."
Therefore humble yourselves under the mighty hand of God, that He may exalt you in due time, casting all your care upon Him, for He cares for you.
Be sober, be vigilant; because your adversary the devil walks about like a roaring lion, seeking whom he may devour. Resist him, steadfast in the faith, knowing that the same sufferings are experienced by your brotherhood in the world.

DISCUSSION

• Why do you think Satan uses pride to attack believers?

• What is God's reaction to pride?

• What are the two sides of the formula for glory?

ACTIVATION

- What would it look like for you to give God the praise and glory He deserves?

- Ask God, "Have I robbed You of any glory through my words or actions?"

- Ask yourself, "How can I live my life as Jesus did and refuse to allow pride to enter my heart?"

OVERCOME DISCOURAGEMENT AND ACHIEVE YOUR DESTINY

INTRODUCTION

Every person will go through times of discouragement, but we can all choose to encourage and strengthen ourselves in the Lord. David made a conscious decision to trust in God's goodness and faithfulness while God forged his character and developed the qualities in David that he would need to serve as Israel's king.

KEY THOUGHT

Every great man or woman of God must overcome times of darkness and deep discouragement in order to achieve his or her destiny in God.

KEY VERSES

1 Samuel 30:1–8

Now it happened, when David and his men came to Ziklag, on the third day, that the Amalekites had invaded the

South and Ziklag, attacked Ziklag and burned it with fire, and had taken captive the women and those who *were* there, from small to great; they did not kill anyone, but carried them away and went their way. So David and his men came to the city, and there it was, burned with fire; and their wives, their sons, and their daughters had been taken captive. Then David and the people who *were* with him lifted up their voices and wept, until they had no more power to weep. And David's two wives, Ahinoam the Jezreelitess, and Abigail the widow of Nabal the Carmelite, had been taken captive. Now David was greatly distressed, for the people spoke of stoning him, because the soul of all the people was grieved, every man for his sons and his daughters. But David strengthened himself in the Lord his God.

Then David said to Abiathar the priest, Ahimelech's son, "Please bring the ephod here to me." And Abiathar brought the ephod to David. So David inquired of the Lord, saying, "Shall I pursue this troop? Shall I overtake them?"

And He answered him, "Pursue, for you shall surely overtake them and without fail recover all."

Psalm 23:1–5

The Lord is my shepherd;
I shall not want.
He makes me to lie down in green pastures;
He leads me beside the still waters.
He restores my soul;
He leads me in the paths of righteousness
For His name's sake.
Yea, though I walk through the valley of the shadow of death,
I will fear no evil;
For You are with me;

Your rod and Your staff, they comfort me.
You prepare a table before me in the presence of my enemies;
You anoint my head with oil;
My cup runs over.

DISCUSSION

- If pride is like a whisper, how is discouragement like a shout?

- What are the four secrets to self-encouragement?

- What is the difference between the physical reality and the spiritual reality?

ACTIVATION

- What should you do when you face a physical reality that doesn't line up with God's Word?

- Ask yourself, "Do I expect victory without difficulty or difficulty without victory?"

- Ask the Lord to strengthen and encourage you. He will do it!

USE YOUR FREE WILL TO SERVE THE LORD

INTRODUCTION

David became great because he chose to focus on God, be a worshipper of God, and act on God's faithfulness to champion the cause of those who trust Him. The same call for greatness is for every man and woman created by God and given the privilege and responsibility of living on this earth in the power of His Son.

KEY THOUGHT

Great people use their God-given free will to serve the Lord.

KEY VERSES

Jeremiah 29:11 (NIV)

"I know the plans I have for you," declares the Lord, "plans to prosper you and not to harm you, plans to give you hope and a future."

Jeremiah 1:5 (NIV)

Before I formed you in the womb I knew you,
  before you were born I set you apart;
  I appointed you as a prophet to the nations.

Luke 18:27

The things which are impossible with men are possible
with God.

Matthew 17:20
  If you have faith ... nothing will be impossible for you.

DISCUSSION

- What was the ultimate secret of David's success in becoming great?

- Name several other great men and women in the Bible. What made these people great?

- What is the enemy's worst nightmare for Christians?

ACTIVATION

- What battlefields has God called you to fight on in your life?

- Ask yourself, "Is anything hold me back from the battlefield?"

- Ask God to show you that His plans are always and only for your good.

ABOUT THE AUTHOR

Jimmy Evans is the founder and CEO of MarriageToday, a ministry based in Dallas, Texas, that is devoted to helping couples build strong and fulfilling marriages and families. Jimmy and his wife, Karen, are passionate about marriage, and together, they co-host *MarriageToday* at www.marriagetoday.com.

Jimmy also hosts *The Overcoming Life*, a daily television program dedicated to seeing people thrive in life and in their walk with God. He serves as senior pastor at Gateway Church, a multi-campus church in the Dallas/Fort Worth Metroplex, and as an overseer of New Life Church in Colorado Springs, Colorado.

Jimmy served as the senior pastor of Trinity Fellowship Church in Amarillo, Texas, for 30 years and now serves as the senior elder. During his years of leadership, Trinity grew from 900 active members to over 10,000.

He holds an honorary doctorate of literature from The King's University and has authored more than 16 books, among which are his popular works *The Overcoming Life, Marriage on the Rock, Ten Steps Toward Christ, Lifelong Love Affair, Why Life Hurts, Strengths Based Marriage*, and *I Changed My Mind.*

Jimmy and Karen have been married for 45 years and have two married children and five grandchildren.

A Note on the Type

This book was typeset in Chronicle Text G3. Chronicle Text is a typeface designed by Hoefler & Co. in 2002. A Scotch styled typeface, Chronicle Text blends the best of both Old Style serif fonts and Modern serif fonts. The typeface was originally designed for newspapers and was created in several grades including G3.

Typeset by Nord Compo,
Villeneuve-d'Ascq, France

Printed and bound by Bethany Press International
Bloomington, MN

Interior design by Peyton Sepeda

MORE FROM JIMMY EVANS

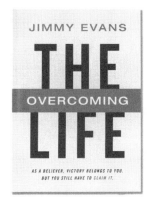 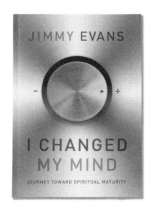 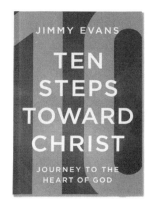

The Overcoming Life (ISBN: 978-1-949399-39-4)

People are waiting for God to fix their problems. However, God will not do for you what He has given you the ability to do for yourself. He has provided all the tools you need to live victoriously. Learn how to overcome rejection, fear, comparison, discouragement, sickness, and doubt.

I Changed My Mind (ISBN: 978-1-945529-32-0)

Becoming a Christian doesn't fix all your problems. Your daily life is still plagued by the fear of failure and weighed down by worry. Bad attitudes keep you stuck. God shows us in His Word a better way to think. If you want to move forward, you must be willing to change your mind.

Ten Steps Toward Christ (ISBN: 978-1-945529-25-2)

Salvation isn't the last step. It's the first. I've accepted Christ—now how do I live as a Christian? Jimmy Evans gives you a map to navigate your new life. He explains how to connect with God, see the Bible as relevant, and find freedom from past hurts.